INDOOR VEGETABLE GARDENING

Improve Your Skills to Grow Up Vegetables at Home. Urban Gardening for Beginners Using Kitchens, Backyards, and Other Indoor Opportunities

Contents

Contents (continued)

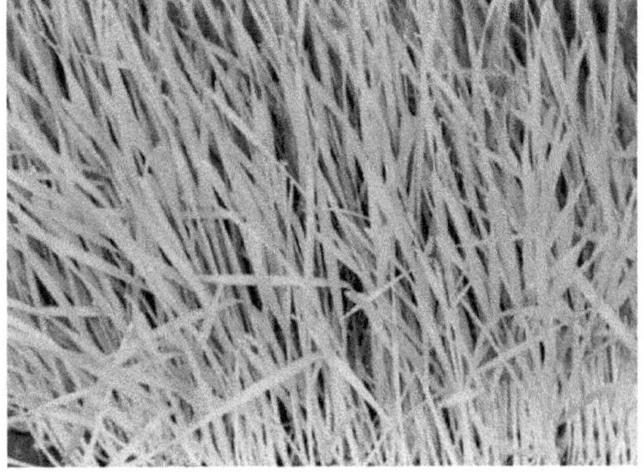

Contents (continued)

Introduction

Growing up in Minnesota, my schools always seemed located across from cornfields and farm stands, but wearily gazing outside during math class was about as close as I got to agriculture. Although my great-grandparents and grandparents were farmers, I grew up in the suburbs, a land of uniform lawns and frozen vegetables, and although I deeply appreciated lazing around in trees and watching bees in the neighbor's garden, I never imagined I'd be spending any time digging, weeding, or talking about compost. The concept of growing food was about as foreign to me as algebra (which I also believed I'd never use).

After a few decades in the business world, that sense of disconnection to my food remained, although I'd expanded into cooking more meals and using more than one spice at a time. It wasn't until I was in my early 40s, though, that I actually grew anything more than an appetite.

Elizabeth (Bossy E) and Karla (Bossy K) in a rare moment of relaxation at their Community Supported Agriculture (CSA) farm, Bossy Acres, in Minnesota.

When people ask how I got into farming, I like to say that I dated my way into it. I met my future partner, Karla Pankow, during a Habitat for Humanity build in Zambia, Africa, and we joke that our relationship started while we had dirt-encrusted hands, so why not continue the tradition from there? The beautiful simplicity of living there—albeit for only a few weeks—stayed with both of us, and we realized that we yearned to create a life focused on sustainability, abundance, gratitude, and plenty of dirt. By launching a farm, Bossy Acres, we're off to an excellent start.

Before we first managed to get into our farmland, though, we began by growing a wealth of crops inside. Winter in Minnesota is notorious for wearing optimists down to a brittle nub, but the more experimentation we did with microgreens, pea shoots, radishes, and other tasty vegetables, the more we felt like we were extending summer into our house. As the snow buried the cars outside, we harvested wave after wave of tiny, delicious greens that kept us busy until we could find some fields to till—or at least break into the raised beds in our backyard garden in Minneapolis.

Microgreens and other indoor edibles do more than simply feed the body. They add color and texture to the interior of your home, and watching them grow is an exciting adventure for kids and adults alike.

The experience went against everything I'd believed for most of my life: that indoor vegetable growing was for experts who possessed deeply green thumbs, and that anything edible raised inside a house had to be grown in some extensive, costly system. Most of all, I thought having a little two-bedroom bungalow in the city was a huge drawback because I didn't have an expansive kitchen with tons of natural light, or a finished basement with space for rows upon rows of grow lights.

Fortunately, through several seasons of indoor growing, I came to see that there are plenty of options when it comes to in-home "farming." Nutrient-rich microgreens, sprouted alfalfa and broccoli, even beets and mushrooms—with the right mix of light, airflow, water, and attention, all can flourish as easily as houseplants.

In this book, you'll learn the basics of indoor growing, get tips on specific "crops," and troubleshoot some common indoor growing issues so that you can easily get started on the leafy, delicious path of in-home gardening. Starting with planning your space, and finding the right area in your home (usually the kitchen, but not always), you can transition to planting, soil conservation, water usage, airflow management, and all those other zesty strategies that go into being an in-home gardener.

Bossy Acres, the Community Supported Agriculture farm operated by Elizabeth and Karla, relies heavily on volunteer field work from CSA members who enjoy getting their hands dirty.

Also included are some ideas on preparing your hard-earned bounty. For several years, I focused so much on growing vegetables that I neglected educating myself on how to actually eat them. Yet, it's hugely important to make food prep into a part of any gardening strategy. That's why I'm just as likely to be pickling, fermenting, and chopping as I am weeding, transplanting, and harvesting. There are certainly times where I plant a certain type of vegetable or fruit just to see if it can be done (I'm looking at you, artichokes), but at the same time, I make sure to be prepared if my ambitious schemes end up working.

A jar full of a blend of spicy microgreens is weighed and prepared to be sent out for sale at a local farmer's market.

A kitchen-window herb garden with good light can yield plants nearly as big as if they were grown outdoors.

Even if your in-home garden is just one plant, seeing a beautiful edible like Swiss chard thriving in your kitchen will give you the confidence to expand and try more new plants in new places.

In short, *Indoor Kitchen Gardening* is about creating a sense of play and nourishment. There's a certain thrill that comes with seeing seeds begin to pop into their first leaves, and if you're wearing your pajamas at the time, that excitement can feel doubled. Although there are some challenging projects wedged into these pages, much of the book is devoted to easy growing practices, so indoor gardening feels more like a fun journey than a daunting task.

It doesn't matter if you're crammed into an urban apartment with one fern balanced on the fire escape or pondering how to use a lovely greenhouse space in your new farmhouse, anyone can use these simple tricks and techniques to develop garden abundance. Let the adventure begin.

Windowsills are built for potted herbs, which make a delightful accompaniment to your favorite pottery and containers.

A few pots of edibles around the house can add up to a significant garden. Here, celery and red sail lettuce share a bench.

A bit of tough-to-reach countertop can be put to use in the highly productive task of supporting your in-home garden. Depending on your conditions, you may not even need to supply supplemental light, heat or ventilation at all.

(ABOVE) A tray full of radishes is ready to be harvested at just a couple inches tall. The development of the second leaf pair is a good sign that most micros are harvestable. (RIGHT) Any spot in your house where you have had success growing typical houseplants is a good candidate for growing edibles. Some good sunlight is a key ingredient for most plant species—edible or not.

PART ONE

Growing Edibles Indoors

Living in the Midwest, I've often dreamed of growing tropical fruits in my dining room, imagining a stretch of mangoes and papayas juxtaposed against the snow-sliding-sideways view of a February afternoon. The kitchen would become a tangle of vines, lush with colorful blooms and quirky vegetables, and I'd be able to pick my breakfast while the morning coffee brews.

Theoretically, with the right conditions, I should be able to achieve at least a fraction of that daydream. For example, it's likely that I could grow a dwarf Calamondin orange tree, which is reputed to be hearty to 20 degrees Fahrenheit, or opt for an avocado tree sprouted from a pit, waiting the four to six years it takes for the new plant to bear its own fruit.

I did attempt to achieve the somewhat impossible once, trying to grow my own loofah plant, even though I knew Minnesota is far out of the loofah's zone. I managed to get it about 5 feet tall, with luscious, broad leaves and plenty of potential, but it never fruited, only kept spinning its tendrils around curtain rods and houseplants. When the project resulted in more pruning than loofah harvesting, I came to an important realization: indoor growing is a pursuit that can be zesty and ambitious, but when it begins to feel like an overwhelming chore, it might be time to scale back. Most of all, I determined that indoor growing is best when it starts with a plan.

Turning your home into an orangery with fresh oranges and lemons growing in abundance is a lovely dream, but you'll have better luck if you start with a more practical plan and build on your successes.

THINKING AHEAD

It's ridiculously easy to become overcommitted and enthusiastic, especially when perusing seed catalogs. Some of the dreariest parts of gardening—weeds, rabbits, squirrels, more weeds, birds, and did I mention weeds?—are eliminated with a kitchen counter brimming with herbs, microgreens, lettuces, and edible flowers. So, some people tend to jump in and place a seed order that wouldn't be out of place for a five-acre hobby farm.

Before hitting "send" on that order, though, take a moment to think about what you really want to grow, and what it will add to your current growing mix (if you have one going).

Creating a plan might seem like it would take the fun out of the adventure of indoor growing, but I've found that the opposite is true. By understanding why I'm planting a specific "crop" and

how I'm going to use that vegetable or herb in the future, I've been able to stay on top of my projects and very little goes to waste. I may not have tropical fruits crawling toward the ceiling, but I don't have guilt pangs from overgrown plants that have to be carted grudgingly out to the compost pile, either.

Similarly, it helps to have a strong sense of timing. Understanding when certain plants will mature and planning accordingly can be helpful for staying on top of multiple growing projects without feeling like you're now a greenhouse manager.

Once you have a plan in place—even if it's a rough idea of what you want to grow—then it's easier to take a look at other factors like space, lighting, containers, etc., with a view toward creating the best conditions for your indoor growing adventures.

For those just starting on the indoor growing path, it's much easier to choose projects/plants based on a few basic questions:

- *What do you hope to gain?* If you want a crop of year-round herbs that keep your meals spicy and seasoned, think about which herbs you might use the most, and focus on those. If you're looking to boost the nutritional profile of your dishes and add flavor, consider microgreens, pea shoots, or other nutritionally dense plants that take up minimum room and deliver abundant health benefits.

- *How ambitious do you want to be?* Certain plants like tomatoes, mushrooms, and potatoes aren't always easy to grow inside, but it can be done. As long as you're taking on projects like that with a sense of play and excitement, then full speed ahead, fellow grower. But if you've never grown so much as a cactus inside and suddenly want to make the leap to indoor tomatoes, you might want to add a few more baby steps into your plan. For instance, start with a reasonably sized container of herbs and once you've mastered the art of watering, pest control, and succession planting, move on to swooning over those heirloom tomato seed descriptions.

- *What's your vacation schedule like?* A "quick trip" or holiday plans have derailed many of my indoor growing projects in the past. As much as I appreciate the kindness of friends who offer to water and prune, I've found it's better for me if I add vacation time into my growing plan and take a break during those times. This seems to be especially prudent when I'm growing a wide array of vegetables. No housesitter wants an elaborate 30-item list of instructions about how to deal with baby carrots, lettuces, microgreens, and mushroom bags while I'm ordering another beer from the cabana server.

- *Are you looking for indoor-only growing, or transfers between the kitchen and outdoor garden?* Many gardeners extend their growing seasons by bringing some plants inside when the weather begins to cool. Herbs, in particular, are a favorite for this transfer since many can thrive fine indoors over the winter, and then go back out in the garden in the spring. If this is your goal, then that's great, but you'll need to tweak your planting mix accordingly. There are certain plants—like cilantro, for example—that simply don't do very well in making the transition. So, when choosing what to grow in your indoor space, do some research on what does best going from outdoors to indoors.

FIND YOUR SPACE

Although this book is called *Indoor Kitchen Gardening*, there are many instances where a kitchen isn't the ideal spot in the house for vegetable or herb growth. Also, the kitchen might be perfect during a certain time of year, especially during cooler months when plants can use the ambient heat of that room, but less suited for growing in other seasons.

For example, I've found that my trays of microgreens do very well in the kitchen during the autumn, when temperatures begin edging toward frost, but suffer in that room during the summer because the south-facing windows heat up the space too much. In those warmer months, the micros thrive in the basement, where I can control the light and air more easily, and avoid the humidity that makes growing more challenging.

Tomatoes and peppers, however, love the heat. Putting them by a large kitchen window in the middle of summer allows them to thrive, but placing them in a basement or cool attic space requires an exhausting amount of control measures to make sure they're happy. In other words, it's likely that your home has the right spot for whatever you have in mind; you just have to find out where that space might be.

A quiet cornet in a living room can be used as a garden or nursery. Here, seedlings are coaxed along under an LED light until they are strong enough to be transplanted into bigger containers and scattered throughout the house.

You wouldn't want to put a recliner or a desk in the small space between these doors, but a shallow shelf filled with garden plants fits the space very nicely.

(ABOVE) A healthy tray of microgreens or shoots can do a lot to improve the view of a window that looks out on a dreary area, such as a garage. (RIGHT) Basements typically offer a wealth of utility space for raising your indoor crops. All that's needed is a decent grow light and perhaps some supplemental heat.

You can't do better than natural sunshine when it comes to providing a light source for starting and growing your edible indoor garden plants. But do be aware that too much sunlight will damage some more delicate plants.

Light

For many indoor growers, some form of artificial light will come into play (more on that later), but for maximum efficiency and sustainability, utilize natural light as much as possible.

As a general rule, south-facing windows are preferred because they allow for abundant light, but depending on where you're located in the country, this could be a benefit or a drawback. Light streams in, but heat does, too. Placing some plants in direct sunlight during the hottest part of a summer day, especially without proper airflow, can cook them instead of bolstering growth.

When selecting a site for growing, look for one that allows for natural light, but can also be shaded in some way. This might be as easy as picking a window that has an awning outside that blocks the sun during the middle of the day, or placing plants on a shelf that gets indirect sunlight. Most likely, if you've noticed good results with existing houseplants, you've found some good spots already, but keep in mind that vegetables, herbs, and fruits need extra care like airflow and pest management.

Choosing a spot with natural light isn't mandatory, but it does cut down on the amount of work you'd have to put in for creating an all-artificial-light system. In my own grow space, I use sunlight as much as I can, by lining up plants on a window-level shelf in my south-facing kitchen and dining room, and then supplement with artificial lights in the winter.

Airflow

Unlike many houseplants, indoor edibles need some type of airflow in order to grow properly. When I first started growing, I didn't realize the importance of this factor, and quickly saw the results of my knowledge gap: molding seeds, struggling starts, no germination, and bugs that seemed to come out of nowhere.

Air circulation helps to mimic outdoor conditions, helping plants to grow in a robust way while minimizing the risk of bacterial issues and pest problems. In my space, I'm fortunate enough to have a cross breeze from windows on two sides of my kitchen, but I still utilize small fans for days when there isn't much wind.

In areas like basements or attics, which can get stagnant pretty quickly, it's especially important to create better airflow. Check out the air circulation section later in this chapter for more in-depth strategies once you've chosen your primary growing space.

A small desk fan can create enough ventilation for a few potted plants.

Room to Grow

Here's some bad news: you can't grow twenty different kinds of herbs on a three-foot space in a kitchen. Believe me, I wish someone had told me that a few years ago.

Like plants out in a field or in an outdoor raised bed, indoor plants need space apart from each other to stretch out. With the exception of microgreens and shoots, which are harvested during the first stage of growth and don't need ample room to expand, most indoor plants benefit from at least some breathing room. Herbs and many types of vegetables can be cozy, but they shouldn't be crowded.

When picking your growing spot and making a plan, create a rough sketch of where each pot or container will go, to give yourself a visual representation of your indoor garden. When it begins to feel like a game of Tetris, consider scaling back on the number of plants, in favor of giving the top contenders a better shot at growth.

To contain mess and water runoff, many indoor farmers move their plants to the sink area for watering and then return them.

If you plant your in-home garden near a water source, such as the kitchen sink, you'll have the option of bringing the plants to water. The main reason this is preferable is that it eliminates the risk of spilling water all around the plants set up throughout the home.

Water/Drainage

Thanks to the breadth of container types available, water and drainage isn't usually a major issue, but it should be considered with plants like microgreens, which have very specific watering needs. Locating those type of plants in a kitchen usually makes the most sense, since it's a few steps from a sink, where plants can be placed to drain or soak.

Another popular spot for just that reason is the bathroom, where the humidity levels can boost the health of some types of plants, usually those that grow in more humid zones. Dwarf citrus trees, for example, can thrive in a bathroom as long as there's enough air circulation and some natural light.

When considering the bathroom as a growing area, though, there are several notes of caution. One comes from my plumber, who's also an avid gardener: Don't soak plants in the bathtub of old houses, unless you want to be asked why you have vermiculite in your drains. Also, bathrooms tend to have the lowest level of light in the house, so some form of artificial light might be necessary.

Finally, think about all the product types you use in the bathrooms: spray-on deodorant, hair spray, perfume and cologne, talcum powder, and so on. Everything that goes airborne will affect the plants you keep in that room, and while that might be fine for house-plants, keep in mind that you'll be consuming the edible plants at some point.

Humidity

Much like air circulation, humidity control is crucial when dealing with indoor growing. In some situations, like seed sprouting, abundant humidity can be very beneficial, but in others, such as pea shoot growing, it can make once-robust stems droop and fade.

Because of this, you may want to choose one spot in the house for seed starts—the bathroom, for example, or a sunny porch—and another for the majority of growing. This two-location approach allows you to develop a greenhouse space that can be better protected against pests, bacteria, and other issues that might affect tender seedlings. It's not always necessary to pick a greenhouse area that's hot and humid, but being able to control humidity in the area, either through plastic sheeting or individual domed lids for pots, can be helpful for making sure that plants get the best start possible.

Pets & Pests

Sometimes, these can be the same thing. Although indoor systems benefit from being protected by outdoor critters like squirrels, rabbits, and chipmunks, one cat can become a mini-Godzilla to a burgeoning kitchen garden's Tokyo.

In our house, which is ruled unconditionally by two dogs, all we need to do is shut the basement door or move pots onto a counter instead of the floor. For other indoor growers with more wily pets like cats, the strategies may have to be more elaborate. I've seen a number of anti-kitty systems cobbled together by other indoor growers, and they can be impressive. Wire screens, large rocks, plastic mesh, repurposed bookshelves: suddenly, a once-simple indoor growth space looks like a kid's fort in the woods.

When choosing a space in the house, it's helpful to find a room that can be sectioned off easily, without scrap lumber becoming involved. This might be a kitchen where a swinging door is shut during the day, or a guest room that's already off-limits to pets.

In terms of true pests, this is far trickier. The aroma of fresh seeds can be compelling for critters like mice, and even houses that never had mouse problems before might be breached because of the new buffet you're creating. In the homes where I've lived, I've found that this is a problem mainly in unfinished basement spaces, and often during the colder months. Because of this issue, I don't grow in that type of area between September and April as a general rule. If that's the only space available, I mouse-proof all areas of the gardening area with as much creativity and kindness as I can muster. Fortu-

If it's green and growing, the chances are pretty good that cats and other pets will want a nibble or two.

nately, I haven't seen a problem in any upstairs spaces like a kitchen or dining room, perhaps because the dogs are overly enthusiastic about seeing small creatures as new best friends.

There will be more, much more, about handling pests and insects in other parts of the book, but for now, it's best to try and choose a space that seems protected already. That can go a long way toward preventing anything other than you from eating your garden produce.

A custom-made cage of poultry netting (otherwise known as chicken wire) can be fashioned around plants and containers to provide a layer of protection from curious pets. This may help, but on the downside, most pets are persistent enough to defeat this strategy and the cage definitely detracts from the loveliness of your indoor garden. Controlling access to the room or perhaps a few sessions at obedience school are better long-term solutions.

One of the greatest advantages to small-scale, in-home gardening is that many of the items you need to get started can be found lying around in most homes, looking for something to do.

Shape is an important consideration when choosing containers. Oblong and rectangular ones are quite useful.

GETTING STARTED

Now that you've chosen a few prime spots in your house, it's time to create an optimal growing area that will be so amazing it will triple your dinner party invitee list, just so you can show it off in a faux-casual manner. "Oh, this space in the kitchen? Yes, I just thought I might grow some salad mix and herbs for tonight's dinner…you don't do that too?"

While practicing your humble-yet-talented gardener expression, here's what you should pick up to create a workable, efficient growing space that will lead to potluck ingredients galore: containers, soil, shelving, lights, fans/air, and of course, seeds or transplants. Let's break it all down.

Even though you can repurpose about anything you can imagine as a planting container, there is something to be said for the utility of purchased items made for planting compared to an old rubber boot. Plastic plant trays with drainage panels are not expensive.

Containers

The breadth of container options is limitless; I've seen indoor vegetables grown in children's old sand buckets, retired purses, worn-out boots, tackle boxes, partially broken drawers, wicker baskets, even a rolling luggage bag that lost its top. Repurposing unused items that are just taking up space in the basement is a fun idea, and it works well for certain kind of projects, but there are a few items to keep in mind when digging through the junk room:

Root depth

Every vegetable, fruit, or herb will have a certain root depth that it needs. Even though it's likely that you won't be attempting to grow deep-rooted plants like asparagus or artichokes (both of which have roots that extend at least 2 feet down), it's helpful to think about how much room you really need.

For microgreens, for example, harvest is done so early in the plant's growth stage that roots barely need any depth. In fact, some people grow them without soil at all, on algae-infused mats that provide nutrients and support growth up to a few inches in height. As a fun kid's project, you could grow microgreens in a bottlecap, or a teacup saucer, anything that can be gently watered and tended for about a week.

Most of the other candidates for indoor growing, though, do need some

It may not be the ideal container for microgreens, but it sure is cute. The wisp of micros growing in this bottlecap demonstrate one thing quite clearly: you can grow microgreens in just about anything.

room for the roots to expand properly. For most vegetables, most of the root mass is within the top 6 inches of soil, so choose a container that can be aerated properly—no small-mouth jars, for instance, or other items that prompt soil compaction—and are reasonably sized for the project. You could choose a large, deep pot for small carrots, for example, but you'd end up using far more soil than you need.

So, choosing a container should have a sense of economy about it: Pick one that gives you room for root growth, but doesn't lead to soil waste.

Drainage

Most likely, you already have plenty on hand if looking for repurposed options, but if you're shopping around at garden stores, consider containers that allow for drainage.

These containers have either a single hole in the bottom of the pot, or several small slits that stretch along the expanse of a tray or pot. Although I love the idea of repurposed containers, and I have a stack of potential candidates in my basement, I usually opt for rectangular trays with drainage slits.

Not only do these types of containers let me accidentally overwater without too much risk of mold, they also allow me to water a plant by setting the whole tray or pot into a sink filled with a few inches of water. For certain

Commercial growing trays normally have drainage slots, which is important for growing indoors. But of course you must set the planting tray into a liner tray to keep the water from running everywhere.

vegetables, especially if they're suffering from overwatering issues or leaf problems, "bottom watering" in this way is particularly helpful. Also, very dense plantings, such as a heavily planted pea shoot tray, benefit from this strategy. The roots can reach the moisture that they need without adverse effects on the upper plant.

There are some plants that don't need this kind of care (usually drought-resistant houseplants) but the majority of vegetables, shoots, herbs and other edibles benefit greatly from the aeration that comes as a result of drainage.

That's not to say that you can't take that antique lunchbox from middle school and turn it into a charming indoor gardening option—however, if plants seem to be struggling in that container due to root rot, then it may be time to go with better drainage strategies.

Material

Many repurposed items are fine in terms of their material—old rubber boots keep the moisture in the soil, metal children's wagons make a nice mobile container, etc.—and many can be modified for drainage by drilling a few holes in the bottom.

One note of caution, though: keep in mind that you'll be eating whatever grows in these containers, so if you're utilizing a cool, retro oil can, you'll have to be diligent in removing all traces of the oil before you plant. Even then, I would be reluctant to utilize that container unless it was my only option.

Any kind of container that seems suspect to me in terms of potentially toxic substances gets scratched off my list. It may seem like farm chic to plant in a rusty wheelbarrow, for instance, and it would be fine for non-edible plants, but I'm hesitant to expose the plant to rust, old chemicals, and other dangers because those issues may affect plant growth, but most importantly, those chemicals would be on my dinner plate, albeit in a small amount.

Plastic and terra cotta pots are two of the most readily available types. Each has its pluses and minuses when it comes to growing edibles indoors.

Some containers are more porous than others. Terra cotta pots, for example, draw moisture from the soil, so they require more frequent watering. Here are some other benefits and challenges of common container types:

- *Plastic:* For most of my growing, I lean toward plastic even though it's not the most attractive or durable solution. These types of trays and pots are my preference because they're lightweight, stackable when not in use, generally quite cheap (or free, if you know a bunch of gardeners who are constantly trying to downsize), and easily modified with additional drainage holes. That said, they are still a petroleum-based product, so they're not the most environmentally friendly option available. I try to minimize my non-green impact by reusing them as much as possible, though.

- *Polystyrene:* Although I don't use many white polystyrene foam boxes myself, I've seen numerous examples of successful growing with these. The trick is to find food-grade containers, but if you live in an area with any kind of supermarket diversity, it just takes a few phone calls to gather a nice collection. Most grocers, and all fishmongers, use these boxes but they have very limited re-use, so you'd be keeping them out of landfills. The foam provides excellent insulation, and it's easy to drill drainage holes in the bottom. The appearance is a drawback, but many people paint them so they look less like a Styrofoam cooler.

- *Stone:* Most of these containers will likely be outside, since the largest drawback is weight. Smaller stone pots, though, can be a good option because they have a nice amount of heat insulation and are definitely very durable.

- *Terra cotta/Clay:* In addition to being more porous, these pots can be prone to cracking when soil freezes. That's not a huge issue for indoor growing, but if you're storing them in a garage when they're not in use, be sure to empty the soil from them first. A more serious issue is that clay pots retain heat very effectively, which is great if you have plants that love heat (like peppers or eggplant), but for those that are less fond of long periods of heat, the plant roots can get burned. In general, though, these types of pots are visually appealing, fairly inexpensive, and have good drainage.

- *Wood:* For many indoor growing spaces, wood is a nice choice because these containers can look amazing, especially with weathered wood (achieved by exposing it to actual weather, so throw a new containers outside for a few months). But wood can also be problematic when it comes to food safety—some containers are treated with very harsh chemicals to keep the wood from molding or rotting, and those toxins can leach into your edibles. Older containers in particular may have been treated with chemicals that leach arsenic into the soil. A good solution that I employ often is to put another pot inside the wooden planter, especially if the leaves will drape over the side to hide the gap between planter and pot. It's possible to seal the container with a good food-grade choice as well, such as a mineral oil and beeswax combination, or a soy sealer (brands include SoySeal or SoyGuard). Just be sure to avoid any conventional wood sealers, because they're chock full of chemicals that don't play well with edibles.

Basically, there's no single, perfect container type that works fantastically well for indoor vegetable and herb growing. Instead, choose a container mix based on what's safe for edible plants, attractive in your kitchen or other growing space, and easily watered.

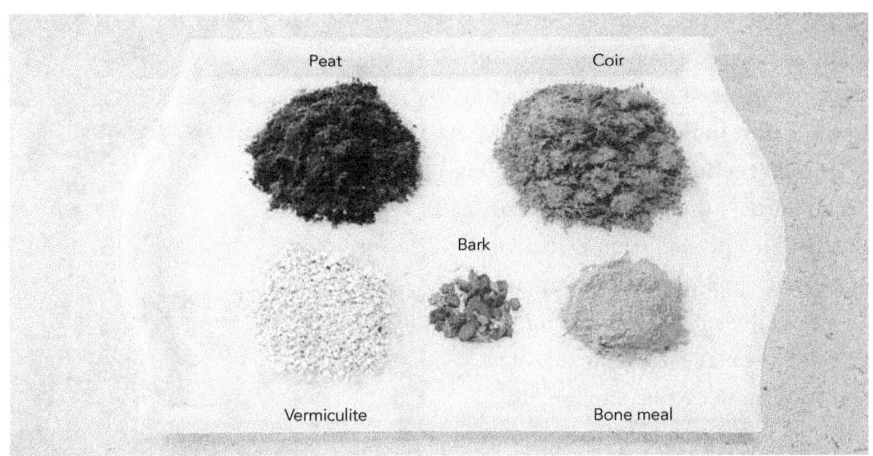

Many indoor growing media blends contain no soil or compost. A suitable media can be made from a blend of peat, coir, vermiculate, bark, and bonemeal.

Soil

Among the many variables that come with in-home growing, the importance of your soil mix can't be overemphasized. Seriously, your soil can make all the difference between healthy, vibrant, nutrient-dense vegetables and sickly, non-germinating, pale plants.

When I first started indoor growing, I thought: dirt is dirt, right? I can just go in my backyard, get a shovel full of the stuff, and I'm on my way. Forget the trip to the garden store and those fancy bags of soil—vegetables grow in dirt outside all the time, so obviously those soil mixes are a scam. This was followed about a week later by an exclamation of: hey, where did all these bugs come from? And about a month later by: hmm, I wonder why nothing is growing?

Very well-prepared soil that's geared toward indoor growing isn't a scam, and it's not optional. Homes and apartments tend to be drier than the outdoors, and putting plants in a container gives them less room and fewer nutrients than they'd have outside, even in a raised bed. Because of that, you need soil that's well aerated, yet able to retain enough moisture to foster growth.

If you use soil from the outdoors—even lovingly mixed with compost—drainage and aeration are almost always impacted, leading to poor growth, if you're lucky enough to get any growth at all. Often, garden soil is higher in nitrogen as well, which is fabulous for an outdoor garden, but when packed into a small space, it acts like a welding torch to your plant's roots.

Also, bugs. I think I could grow plants in a sealed room, ventilated with the purest filtered air, and handled only by volunteers in HAZMAT suits, and I would still get bugs if I used garden soil. That's because the insects are already in the dirt, so it doesn't matter what kind of pristine conditions you set up in your house, you're still giving them a free taxi ride to an all-day seedling buffet.

With those caveats, though, it's true that some people can pull it off. My partner, Karla, seems to be able to grow anything anywhere, and I believe she could nurse along a mango tree successfully through a Minnesota winter. She has the touch. But, because I don't, I tend to be more deliberate in how I set up my space for growing and with that in mind (in case you tend to be one of those people, too), here are some tips for choosing good soil:

Vermiculite is a mica rock that is ground and then heated up until it explodes like popcorn. It has no nutritional value for plants, but it prevents the growing media from compacting.

- Some of the best options for indoor growing don't contain soil at all, but are instead a combination of materials like peat, bone meal, coir fiber (ground up coconut hulls), bark, and vermiculite.

- That last item can be particularly useful—vermiculite is a silicate that's fluffy and pebble-shaped. It helps to promote fast root growth, anchor young roots, boost mois-ture retention, and assist germination. You'd look for horticultural vermiculite, as opposed to other types that are used for shipping chemicals or enriching concrete. Many potting soils already have vermiculite added, however, and you can tell by the distinctive white, chalky flecks distributed throughout the mix. If you're whipping up your own mix, consider blending compost and vermiculite.

This seems like a good point to climb atop my soapbox about organics. I love the view from up here. Simply put, we farm organically, and we believe deeply in creating a sustainable agriculture system, and that extends just as much to the cilantro growing on my kitchen counter as it does to the heirloom tomatoes out in our fields. So, I do my research on planting mixes, and I buy from locally owned greenhouses. Most of the time, this means that I pay more for my potting mix, but also that I feel better about what it contains.

I'm always keenly aware that what I grow will end up in my body, and a few extra dollars upfront is worth it to me to know that I'm getting as close to chemical-and-toxin-free as possible.

Just because something is labeled as "organic," though, doesn't make it natural and sustainable.

Recently, I went against my own eco-friendly policies because I was in a planting emergency (they really do happen!) and needed potting mix quickly. I opted for a stop at a big box retailer and got a suspiciously cheap mix that was labeled organic. Inside, I found a mix that was quite heavy and contained bits of candy wrappers, small wires, glass beads, and other weird garbage.

Since I was in a jam, I used it anyway, and I shouldn't have bothered. The mix was so dense that it turned my trays into mud blocks that wouldn't drain, and nothing germinated. When I dumped them out, the blocks had solidified into nearly unbreakable bricks of soil. Perhaps if I was building a mud house on the frontier, this would have been a valuable moment, but otherwise, it was a waste of time, money, and effort.

Choose a potting mix that is specifically for indoor vegetable and herb growing. These are put together in a way that fosters better drainage, and most of all, contains only a small amount of fertilizers. This is important, because too much fertilizer can burn a plant's roots, especially in smaller containers. I tend to use a compost-and-vermiculite blend for growing, and if it seems like any of my plants are struggling or slow in germinating, then I might turn to fertilizer like bone meal or fish meal, which are both great at maintaining proper soil chemistry without burning the young seedlings. Compost and fertilizer tends to work well together, because each supplies nutrients, especially during the early stages of plant growth.

Step One: measure out about 7 to 8 cups of indoor potting soil or compost mix, and about 2 cups of vermiculite.

Step Two: blend the dry ingredients thoroughly with your hands.

Step Three: add water; depending on how dry the soil is, you'll probably need at least 2 to 3 cups of water, but add it gradually and mix it in until you can squeeze a handful and have a few drops (not a stream) dribble out.

Step Four: test the consistency of the growing medium. It should clump together without too much pressure, but fall apart once you let go of it.

You don't have to make your living room or kitchen feel like a commercial greenhouse to grow edibles indoors. Tasteful wall shelving that's integrated into your room décor does the job, too.

Coated wire shelving is inexpensive, durable and adjustable. It also allows good airflow.

Shelving

Of all the parts of a growing strategy, shelving usually has the most do-it-yourself appearance. I've seen "shelves" cobbled together from old screen doors, repurposed planks of wood on top of cinder blocks (making me recall my early days of college living), and bookshelves that have plants on top and slightly water-warped novels on the bottom.

Basically, it doesn't matter too much what you use, as long as it will support the weight of your plants and you don't mind getting it wet if you need to mist the plants or to put just-watered pots or trays on the shelves.

I've repurposed a wide range of shelving options, from countertop spice racks to old nightstands, and it's fun to root around in the basement and see unused furniture with new, savvy gardener vision. If putting together a system from scratch, though, here are some recommendations as a guide:

- *Consider metal, industrial-style shelving.* This type of unit is usually sturdy, able to be configured easily, and best of all, has a nice degree of openness in the back and sides. Also, steel shelves have an open slat design for each shelf, which helps to increase airflow. Especially handy, these open slats let you hang lights fairly quickly without the kind of drilling or clever DIY effort you'd need for standard wooden bookshelves.
- *Don't put plants on shelves that you love.* This sounds like odd advice, but believe me, any surface will get dirty and wet very quickly. Even when you think you can be extremely careful in keeping the

bottom of the pots and trays dry, you can still get water stains on wood shelves.

- *Think about your lighting options when buying shelves.* We'll dive into lights in the next section, but for now, all you have to remember is that a standard-sized shop light is 4 feet long. If you buy an industrial-type shelving unit that's 48 inches across, and has the open slat design for hanging those shop lights, you'll feel like a pro. At least, that's how I felt after years of weird systems that I patched together, many of them featuring shop lights hanging way past a shelf's edge.

- *Go for adjustable shelving.* Being able to change the height of your shelves is very useful, because plants need different levels of light. It's possible (and recommended) to use the chains that come with shop lights to adjust height of lights, but it's also a nice option if you can reconfigure shelves as well. This comes in handy, too, when using one of the shelves as a storage area for tools, extra pots, a watering can, and other growing supplies. Quick note on storage: if you'll be keeping your seeds on this shelf, make sure to store them in a sealable plastic bin, to lessen the temptation to pests.

Take the edible landscape idea indoors by combining your edibles with houseplants and even cut flowers in your existing shelving and display furnishings.

In general, find a shelving system that allows for a nice amount of light (natural or artificial), gives the plants room to spread out a little, and offers enough space for proper airflow around the plant. As mentioned previously, lack of airflow is one of the biggest causes of nasty issues like mold and disease, so keep it in mind as you're creating your shelving setup.

Also, if you're just starting out, be aware that you may have to move your shelves if your chosen space turns out to be less than ideal. A spot that seems like it would be perfect may end up being too close to the window, or not situated near an electrical outlet for your shop lights, or too cold and damp. Being flexible about placement (here's where the wheeled shelf comes in handy) is all part of the adventure when it comes to indoor growing.

A plug-in shop light with a full-spectrum fluorescent bulb makes a perfect light source for indoor gardening. Look for one that has hanging chains for easy lowering and raising.

Lights

When I teach classes about growing vegetables, microgreens, and herbs indoors, the question of lighting always comes up first, no matter how early I put it into my talk. At this point, I should probably just issue a note of assurance before the introduction: "I promise, you don't need special, expensive grow lights that are hard to find and burn out easily. Really. I promise."

In fact, all you need are full-spectrum fluorescent bulbs, similar to what you see in office buildings. They can be put into standard metal light fixtures that have one bulb in them, and feature small chains on either end for easy placement into a shelving setup.

These are found in any hardware store and are called various names like utility lighting or shop lighting. Occasionally, they go on sale, and this is when you should pounce on them and buy several at a time if you're going to create a shelving unit filled with plants. Otherwise, you can probably get one, with bulb, for under $30 and usually for much less. Thanks to buying bulbs in a bulk contractor pack (also at the hardware store) and a sale on the fixtures, I paid about $10 for each of my lights. That's quite a difference from the LED grow light systems, where a single bulb can be $60.

You may already have proper lighting if you're planning on growing vegetables, herbs, and fruits in your kitchen. Most under-the-counter fluorescent lighting works well for fostering growth, and all you'd need is some type of small block or shelf that brings the plants closer to that light. I have this type of lighting in my kitchen, and I like to grow herbs in smaller pots so that I can use a little shelf that used to hold dried spices.

Beyond that basic setup, there are other lighting options if you have specific growing needs—sometimes, plants need a boost in some way, and that's when you can try playing around with lighting options.

For example, if a plant seems to be spindly or too leggy, you can give it a burst of red or orange light, which stimulates growth and flowering. If the plants are too short or stocky, you can use blue or green light to regulate plant growth or foliage.

Here's a quick guide to your options:

Incandescents

- Used most for low-light, heat-loving houseplants like ferns or vines

  Only about 10 percent of their energy used for light, with the rest used for heat, so they tend to be inappropriate for indoor edibles since they "cook" the plant.

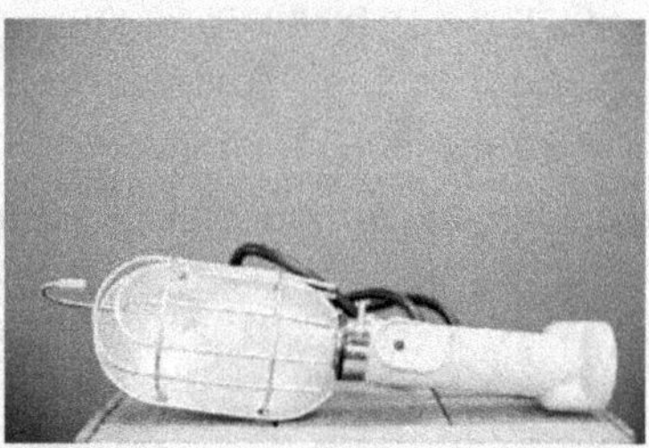

A hanging trouble light with an incandescent bulb emits more heat than light, which isn't necessarily a bad thing for growing plants.

Full-Spectrum Fluorescents

- Best replicates the natural solar spectrum
- Life span of 24,000 hours
- Good choice for year-round growing
- When buying these, look for T8 or T5 bulbs

Full-spectrum fluorescent lighting most often is found with thinner T8 style bulbs like the one above.

Fluorescents

- Two to three times more light than incandescent bulbs for the same amount of energy
- Least expensive option
- Tends to be the most available, especially if you're considering using existing under-the-counter kitchen lighting or shop lights
- Life span of 16,000 to 20,000 hours
- When buying these, most standard is a T12 bulb

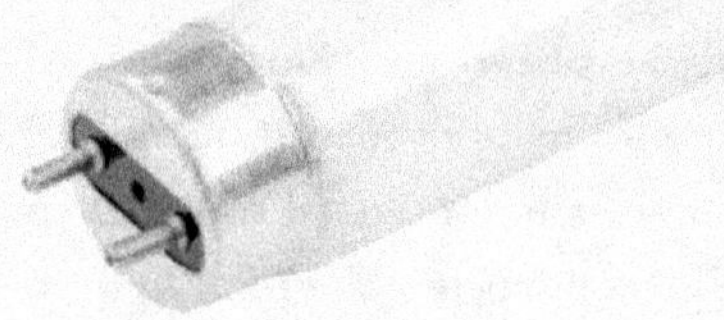

Fluorescent tubes are efficient and available in full-spectrum light models that are intended to replicate natural light as closely as possible. The standard T12 style bulb, like the one above, is by far the most common, but this style is gradually being phased out in favor of more efficient, narrower tubes that operate with an electronic ballast. The T12 works with a magnetic ballast.

High Intensity Discharge (HID)

- More expensive than fluorescents, but twice as efficient
- Can get bulbs that are only red/orange (called MH bulbs) or only blue/green (called HPS bulbs) so you can tweak your growing conditions
- Color of the lights distorts the appearance of plants and grow space; a minor consideration, but some gardeners are put off by the tendency of HID lights to make everyone look jaundiced

Light-Emitting Diode (LED)

- More expensive than fluorescents
- Some bulbs don't require special fixtures, since they're already placed inside panels that can be plugged in.
- Tend to be more appropriate for commercial use

The newest grow light technology is plasma, which purports to be as close to real sunlight as possible. However, I haven't seen one of these systems for under $1,500, so for now, if I want my plants to have more sunlight, I'll just shove them closer to the window.

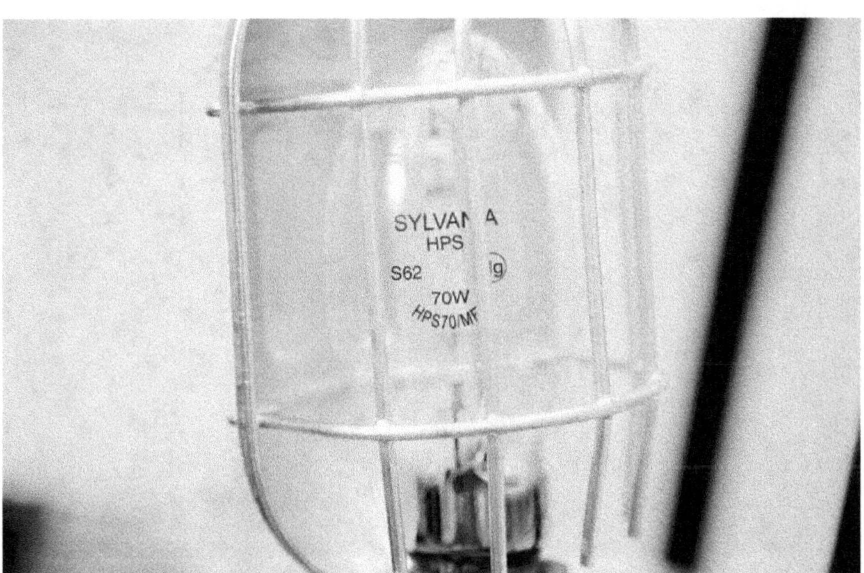

HID bulbs fit into standard sockets, such as this hanging trouble light. Because the bulbs are filled with an inert gas they operate very efficiently.

In general, I prefer the full-spectrum fluorescents because they're affordable and available, but if you want to try an HID or an LED system, then by all means, go for it.

One important note when it comes to lighting: just like people, plants need a night as well as a day. Some growers have tried to boost growth by keeping the lights on at all times, but I've found this creates unnecessary stress on the plants because they don't have time to "sleep." You wouldn't water them with Red Bull, so why would you keep them sleep deprived? A better strategy, I've found, is to turn the lights on in the morning and turn them off about the same time as sunset; in the winter, I'll keep the lights on longer in the evening, but I'll be sure to turn them off before I go to bed.

LED lights are extremely energy efficient and come in an ever-expanding range of sizes and configurations. While any light will do to some extent, you'll get best results from an LED grow light that is designed to emit the complete spectrum of light wavelengths that plants require.

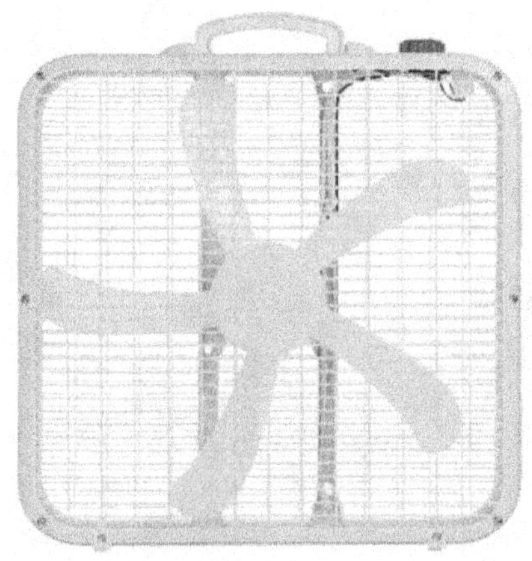

For vegetables grown in our basement I set up two box fans and arranged them so the airstreams would cross, set on low.

Fans/Air

When crops are outside, they get a little blown around by the wind, and this is crucial for more than taking pretty farm pictures of swaying corn and sunflowers. That airflow assists with temperature control, humidity, disease resistance, and oxygen intake. Plants grow stronger from being "stressed" by the wind, and they end up more robust as a result.

Growing plants indoors, you need to find a way to replicate natural conditions—similar to setting up an artificial day for your vegetables and herbs, you also need to create an artificial wind. Fortunately, you can do it on the cheap.

If your plants are near a window and the temperature outside isn't extremely hot or bitingly cold, simply opening the window for a few hours per day can yield enormous benefits.

When plants are in a more enclosed area without a window, it can be trickier to adjust airflow, but certainly not impossible. For vegetables grown in our basement, for example, I set up two box fans and arranged them so the airstreams would cross, set on low. This made the seedlings waver in the "wind," but not get mowed down by the strength of the breeze. The circulation is crucial, because plants don't do well if air is directed in a solid stream in one direction. That would be like taking a hairdryer, putting it on the coolest setting, and aiming it at your seedlings.

In another room, where there was a window on either side but I didn't put the plants close enough to benefit from opening them, I put a fan in each window—one angled toward outside, and one angled into the room. This sets up a simple intake and exhaust system, where fresh air came in regularly and stale air vented out the other side. In order to break up the airflow and create cross-ventilation, I set up a small oscillating desk fan above the plants, at the same level as the intake fan.

If you already have plants in place and are starting to notice any fungal issues or disease problems (like mold), and you've worked to make sure you're

A small desk fan, like this retro-style, oscillating model, is sufficient to provide a light breeze to help keep a small grouping of edibles healthy. Generally, the more your growing conditions mimic the outdoors, the better your plants will do.

not overwatering, chances are good that airflow will be able to help. Buy a few cheap oscillating fans or box fans and set them up so that you can get some ventilation in your growing area during the day, about the same length of time as you have the lights on. If the air seems very stagnant, though—which can happen in an area like a basement—it's fine to leave them on at all times.

In general, the idea is to mimic the low levels of wind that a plant would get while outside. This can help reduce incidence of disease, and make vegetables and herbs heartier.

A sampling of seeds for indoor kitchen gardening includes seeds for growing microgreens as well as sprouting and growing shoots and vegetables.

Seeds

Every winter, it seems that the seed catalogs arrive at roughly the same time, leading to a pile of reading material that always makes me geek out with happiness. I pore over each description, look longingly at the heirloom varieties, and make my (often overly ambitious) plans for the summer. During a part of the year when the only sound seems to be wind and snowplows, the seed catalogs provide a delicious glimpse of abundance.

They're also hugely helpful for indoor growing as well, because beyond the luscious descriptions, these catalogs—both in print and online—provide a wealth of information that can be used to plan a better indoor garden strategy.

Important Information on Buying Seeds

This is what you need to know when choosing seed varieties:

- *Light requirements:* Similar to houseplants, it's useful to know the level of light an edible might require. For example, beets do well with full sun every day, but chard can thrive with some occasional light shade.
- *Seeding depth:* This is usually more important when you're seeding outdoors, but is still worth knowing if you're planting inside so that you don't push the seed too far into the pot and lessen your chances of germination.
- *Plant spacing:* Again, this information is better suited to row gardening or farming, but if you're putting multiple edibles in one pot (such as lettuces or herbs), it's good to know so that you don't crowd out the plants before they've had a chance to establish.
- *Days to maturity:* This is one of the most crucial pieces of info for me, because it can help me gauge when I can expect to harvest. Even with plants that regenerate, like herbs, I like to have a sense of the timeframe from seeding to harvest.
- *Soil and fertilization needs:* Many seed companies will provide acidity level information, which is great if you love to dig into the science of growing, but it's not mandatory to check those levels in order to have a good growing strategy. However, do pay attention to what type of soil works best—loose, well-drained soils are usually recommended for container gardening—and whether you need to use any type of fertilizer. Since nutrient requirements vary widely according to plants, we'll delve into fertilizer needs later in the book when discussing specific crop varieties.
- *Plant management:* Some seed companies do a fantastic job of providing tips on pests, diseases, harvesting, and even storage. Reading through these descriptions can feel like a college agriculture course sometimes, and I've walked away from a seed catalog reading session knowing about things like pirate bugs (not as adorable as they sound).
- *Container gardening suitable:* Because of the rising interest in indoor growing and container gardening outside, seed companies have started putting some great information on their websites. High Mowing Organic Seeds, for instance, has a nice online section about the topic, including suggested varieties, tips on growing, and a "seed collection" of 10 packets that tend to do well in containers.

A quick note on organics here: because we own a farm that's been certified organic, we must buy organic seed, since that's part of the certification process. Beyond that, I'm a fan of organic growing, so even if we didn't have to use those type of seeds for Bossy Acres, I'd still buy them. I believe that organic practices lead to more sustainability, healthier soils, and a better agricultural system in general. Because of that, I think organic seeds are worth the extra cost that's usually involved in purchasing the seeds. You might opt for inexpensive, non-organic seeds instead, and that's cool, no judgment.

I'd just advise you to make sure your seeds are coming from an established source, where you can get the type of growing information that you need. There have been many times that helpful family members have given me seeds from who-knows-where and they hand them over in little plastic bags. "These are hot peppers," one of them will say. "They're really good. I think. They might be sweet peppers, though." That's the extent of the information I receive—they don't know the variety, growing timeframe, potential root depth, or anything else that helps me make a decision in how I grow the plant. So, I usually just end up putting them in my backyard's raised beds, in a grab-bag experimental area that doesn't get much devotion or tending. Sometimes it works out, most times it doesn't.

Another consideration in choosing seeds is whether to opt for heirloom varieties, even though some growers have

Just about any of the seeds you'll use indoors are available as organic or conventional (non-organic). Both work, and while conventional are cheaper and easier to find, choosing organic seeds is a great way to support organic growing practices by voting with your wallet.

found that heirlooms may be less consistent in terms of yield. Still, they're fun for me, because it feels like I'm continuing a tradition and keeping plant variety going. Heirlooms are plants that aren't grown in commercial-scale agriculture, and hail from previous generations. For example, there are only a few potato varieties grown on large-scale farms, which makes it enjoyable for me to choose lesser-grown varieties that might "die out" if it weren't for dedicated growers who keep them going.

Keep in mind that not all heirloom seeds are organic, but if you want both heirloom and organic, there are many options. Take a look in the Resources section of the book for a short list of seed providers that I've found dependable. Basically, seeds are everywhere if you start looking for them; once, I saw a seed rack in the gas station of a small town.

No matter where you obtain your seeds, be sure to store them properly, in a plastic bin with a secure top. This will prevent numerous pest issues, and help to prolong the life of your seeds. For best results, use the seeds within a year or so, and sooner if possible. The older seeds get, the less likely they are to germinate. Sometimes, when I've had seeds around for a while, I create an "anything goes" microgreens mix, since I'll harvest at the first stage of growth anyway. If I want actual vegetables, though, I go with fresh seeds whenever possible.

A small plastic file box makes a great storage container for seed packets. Keep the box in a cool, dry area away from direct sunlight.

Another handy tip: jot down notes right on the seed packet, including when the seeds were purchased. I use the packets for observations as well, noting what might be fast growing or whether a variety proved to be particularly good for one of my vegetable fermentation projects. It's very easy for me to lose track of notebooks, even when I try to store them with my growing supplies. But because I keep my empty seed packets in the same bin as my other seeds, I know where they are, and that one small packet will be rife with information, from both the seed company and my own experience.

Transplants

Although there's a certain thrill with growing from seed—seeing the germination and that first little pop of a plant start never gets old for me—transplants might be more useful for some indoor growing. Particularly if you've had difficulty starting from seed before, or you just want a jumpstart on your growing plan, transplants from a reliable source are a nice way to build your garden quickly.

In some cases, especially for herbs, it makes sense to transfer the plants from an outdoor garden into your indoor growing mix. If you have some robust rosemary outside, for example, there's no need to start rosemary inside from seed since you can just take a cutting off that plant or dig it up completely and plunk it into an indoor pot.

When bringing a plant from outside to inside, make sure to knock as much garden soil off the roots as possible, without damaging the plant. Even if the plant has thrived in this soil for months, there's risk of transferring insects or disease that can affect other parts of your indoor garden. Also, outdoor soil doesn't drain well when used in pots or planters, so use a potting mix instead.

Another consideration is the transition temperature. Whenever you move a plant from an indoor environment to an outdoor space, you need to make that shift gradual so that the plant has time to adjust, and the same consideration is helpful for bringing the plant in the other direction. Re-pot outside, if possible, or in a cooler space like a garage. Water well, and then plan on leaving the plant in a transitional area for a few days—garage, porch, enclosed deck, anyplace where the temperature is slightly warmer than outside. If available, make one more transfer before bringing the plant inside.

For example, if I were to re-pot an herb from outside, I'd put it in the garage first with the windows open for better airflow, then after a few days I'd transfer the plant to my enclosed porch, near one of the open windows in there. Finally, I'd bring the plant inside after a week to 10 days, making sure to water thoroughly in order to aid the transition. Like many people, plants don't respond well to sudden changes, so taking a gentle approach is always helpful.

If using transplants from a garden store or farmers' market, then it's fine to bring them directly inside. The plants have already had a chance to be in an environment that's cozier than outside in the ground, and they're prepared for indoor growing.

Whether your transplants come from a store or your own outdoor space, also be sure to pot them up in a

Transplanting a new seedling from a nursery can be done simply by setting it into your container and filling around the roots with growing medium. If you are transplanting a small plant or seedling that you've grown outdoors, remove as much soil as you can from the root system to minimize the chance of introducing disease.

container that's free of disease. Using a new pot or tray works for this, but you can utilize what you have on hand as long as you make sure that the container's previous tenant didn't have any issues. If you're throwing out a plant because it never thrives, for example, or seems to always have disease problems, it's best to recycle that container as well—even if the plant is gone, the disease can linger, so it's better (and more economical) to be safe.

Miscellaneous Growing Supplies

Even when you're working to keep costs in line, it seems there's always just one more thing to buy at the garden center. Maybe you want to try some coconut coir to mix into your soil to improve drainage, or you're loving those glass watering bulbs that can be stuck into a pot and left for days. When I'm trying to stick to a budget, I try to avoid going to the garden center for anything because I feel like one of the kids who saw Willy Wonka's candy garden for the first time.

In order to properly outfit your little growing space, though, you do need a few supplies, and these come in handy:

- *Automatic light timers.* If you don't want to worry about turning lights on and off during a specific time-frame, these timers are very useful, and they're often fairly inexpensive. I use them when I'm going away for a weekend, or if I'll be busy for a stretch of time and want to reduce my indoor garden maintenance.

- *Heat mats.* Also called germination mats, these are designed to be placed underneath plants so that roots stay warm in cooler areas like basements or drafty corners. They're usually rectangular, and don't have temperature settings; you just roll them out, plug them in, put your pots or trays on top and you're good to go. The low temperature won't burn your plants (unlike, say, a heating pad would) and they do help during the winter months, I've found. Also, if your plants seem slow to germinate, using one of these can provide a

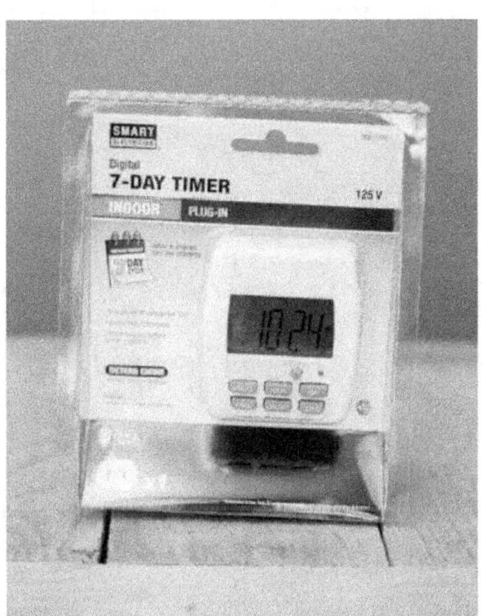

Timers are plugged in to your receptacles and programmed to turn lights on and off (you plug the light into an outlet on the timer body).

Heat mats are placed beneath planting trays to warm the plant roots and to speed up germination in cooler weather.

boost. One caveat: they're usually not cheap, so if you see one on sale, snap it up.

- *Plastic mister bottle.* These are extremely useful, and only cost a few dollars. They can be utilized for an array of growing-related tasks, like spritzing fish emulsion on tomatoes, or spraying a soapy solution on aphid-ravaged plants. During certain times of year, my growing space feels a little drier than other times, so I often mist water over all the plants at least once per day.

- *Small plastic bins/totes.* Usually, I can get these for just a few bucks from places like Target, Family Dollar, or IKEA. Whenever there's a sale, I must look like a professional organizer, because I load up on them, especially ones that are about the size of a shoebox. Put everything in these that you need: scissors, twine, Sharpies, pens, light timers, rubber bands, etc. Also, these bins will be handy for organizing seeds; I tend to use several containers so I can sort seeds according to usage (pea shoot seeds in one bin, microgreens seed in another, and so on). I really wish that the rest of my house was as organized as my indoor gardening space.

Mister bottles come in many forms, from very cheap to professional grade. It's worth investing in a better quality model.

COMMON PROBLEMS

In the rest of this book, I'll dive into details on how to grow specific types of indoor vegetables, herbs, and fruits, but there are common issues that affect most indoor edibles, and it's helpful to know these general concerns before planting that first seed.

Mold

Vegetables, herbs, fruits, and even houseplants are all more susceptible to mold issues than outdoor plants for a number of reasons. They tend to get more water, which can introduce mold spores, and they're sometimes growing in wooden containers, which introduce that water into small cracks in the wood. Humidity, airflow, and poor soil also contribute to mold.

It's quite easy to tell that you have a mold problem, because if you've ever seen a loaf of bread go bad then you know what can happen—a gray or yellowish fuzz begins forming in just one spot and soon it's expanding everywhere. Getting mold on the plant itself is less common, fortunately,

Living indoors does limit the type and number of afflictions that can affect plants, but they are by no means immune from problems such as mold and disease. In most cases, the remedy is more or less water and/or light.

but it does happen if mold on the soil isn't treated in a timely way. Most often, you'll see that telltale fuzz at the base of the plant, or along the container edge.

Prevent mold by watering when the plant needs it, not as a daily (or twice daily) habit. There are many conditions, such as cooler temperatures, when plants don't need as much moisture, so putting plants on an automatic watering schedule can result in dampness, leading to mold. Another problem is inadequate drainage. When this is lacking, plants are sitting in soggy soil, which can lead not just to mold but also insect issues and disease.

Putting the plant in more direct sunlight can be helpful, as well as increasing the airflow or putting the plant near an open window so it can get more fresh air.

There are also chemical fungicides, but I like to consider those as a very last resort since I'm spraying them into my indoor air, even if it's a couple spritzes. Instead, I've had some success with crushing up a clove of garlic and letting it sit in a cup of water for about 15 minutes; then, I put the concoction in a mister, shake thoroughly, and spray on the plants. That method, combined with moving the plant to a sunny spot, often does the trick.

Also, some essential oils can be used as natural mold fighters, including

One homeopathic remedy for abating mold on your indoor plants is to crush a clove of garlic into a cup of water. Let the garlic steep for 15 minutes or so, then transfer the garlic-infused water to a mister and spray the affected plant lightly.

rosemary, cinnamon, and tea tree. Just put a few drops into a cup of water, add to mister, and spray the affected areas—for stubborn mold, you can spray once a week.

No matter what the method used, just be sure to isolate the plant so that the mold doesn't spread to other vegetables, herbs, and fruits.

If mold keeps cropping up—and for some people, it's a scourge that seems to plague their indoor growing efforts on a continual basis—consider switching out your setup completely, especially your soil and containers. It can be pricey to do a total rehaul of your efforts, but a fresh start can help to tackle ongoing mold issues.

Pest Control

As a farmer, and especially as an organic farmer, I'm used to seeing an array of bugs, from flea beetles that feast on my cabbages to Colorado potato beetles that can strip a plant down to sticks in less than a day. Even with the knowledge that we'll be losing part of our crops to insect damage, however, I still feel an elevated sense of injustice about them, as if they're the mean girls in my otherwise peaceful high school lunchroom.

That same smoldering frustration comes up in my indoor growing efforts, but at least my at-home gardening is on a much smaller scale, and so I can actually do something about the situation. The usual suspects for indoor pests include aphids, whiteflies, mites, and mealybugs, all terrifically annoying.

No matter what options you choose, it's smart to gravitate toward non-toxic options. Although I'm obviously a fan of organic methods, this goes beyond my beliefs—conventional pesticide sprays that are designed to be used outside (and usually with respiratory protection) can wreak havoc when used inside where air ventilation is severely reduced.

Also, much like choosing a non-toxic container for planting, keep in

Preventing Disease

Here are a few pest control measures to try on any kind of vegetable, herb, or fruit plant:

- Increase the air circulation by placing a fan nearby or opening multiple windows that allow strong cross breezes.
- Move adjacent plants, especially houseplants, away from your vegetables and herbs—the pests may be targeting one type of plant but end up affecting your whole indoor garden.
- Dip a cotton swab in rubbing alcohol and gently brush the plant's leaves, if the insects are mainly on the top of the plant and aren't too numerous.
- Create a mix of mild liquid soap (like Dr. Bronner's) and water and spray the plants.
- If the outdoor weather is amiable, put the plants outside; if you're dealing with aphids, you may have a hungry ladybug population outside just waiting for this kind of takeout.
- It's possible to buy beneficial insects like ladybugs or lacewings and release them inside your house without causing a rippling effect (in other words, you're not getting a mongoose to handle the snake

that you bought to kill the mice), but keep in mind that this method tends to work best with large-scale pest populations. If you have a sizeable greenhouse area, for example, then it might make sense, but if you've only got a few aphid-infected indoor tomato plants next to your kitchen window, buying a standard order of ladybugs (at least 4,000) seems like overkill, to put it mildly.

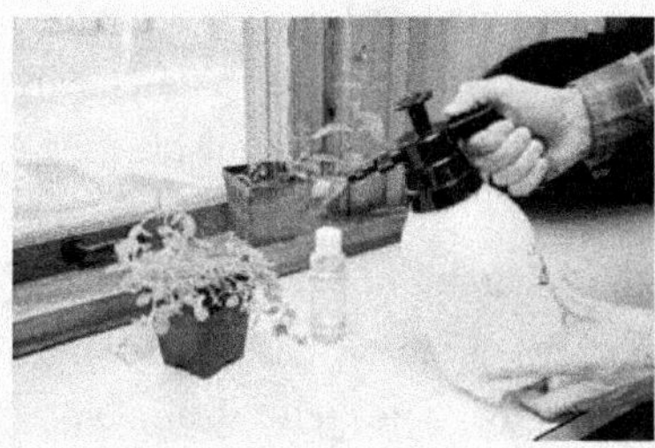

To discourage insects from munching on plant leaves, mix a small amount of mild liquid soap with warm water and lightly spray the plant with a mister. This won't harm the plant but makes the leaves quite distasteful (be sure to wash them before eating them yourselves).

mind that whatever comes in contact with the plant may eventually affect the person or animal who eats it. Personally, I don't like the idea of nibbling on chemical-laden pesticides, even in trace amounts. So, I choose not to go that route. But if you're finding that nothing works whatsoever and you want to try to save the plant from infestation, then at least bring the plant outside if you spray it with conventional pesticide formulas, so that the toxins don't get trapped inside the house.

On a preventative note, carefully inspect any transplants that you're planning to bring inside for indoor growing. If leaves are shiny, or tiny eggs appear in clusters anywhere on the plant, clean it off carefully and leave it outside for a few days if possible to make sure the pests don't hatch into a full infestation.

In terms of other pests, mice can be an issue, too. They tend to appear in older houses, I've found, as well as greenhouse spaces that are attached to kitchens, because those rooms may have air ducts close to the ground. Nearly every greenhouse I've ever visited has mousetraps tucked into the corners, and birds swooping in and out through open windows to steal seeds.

Controlling these pests is very difficult, but not impossible. Some anecdotal evidence suggests that sprinkling peppermint oil around pots and trays is effective, as well as a box-type device called "the tin cat," in which mice can enter but not exit. The ultrasonic devices, however, have been universally panned by nearly everyone I've asked (and believe me, I've had way too many mice discussions in the past few years), and most people just suggest I get a real cat.

Disease Issues

As disheartening as mold or mice are shriveled or mottled leaves, blackened vegetables, or other indications of disease can also be dismaying. Unfortunately, disease can occur even in the best setup, and greenhouse managers are often on a constant state of high alert to try to prevent issues. At our farm, we make sure to wear greenhouse-only boots, and to rinse off any tools or carts that have been in the fields, to prevent diseases from hopping inside from outside.

In a house or apartment, measures like that aren't feasible. You may be transferring disease because you didn't shake off enough of the outdoor soil when repotting herbs from the garden, or your plants might be more susceptible to issues because your care isn't quite what's needed.

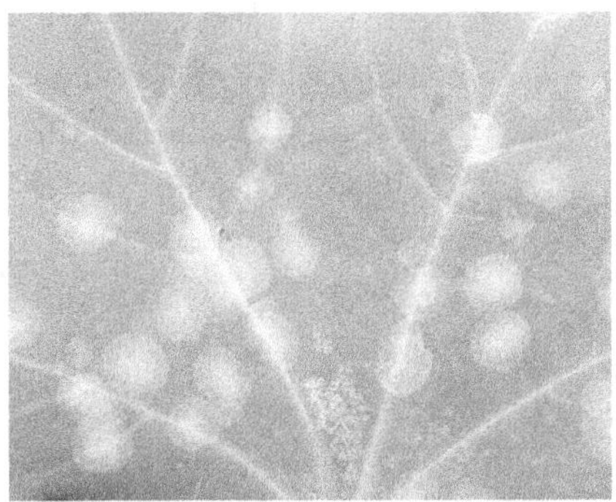

Powdery mildew is one of the more common fungal infections plants experience in agriculture, but it can hit your indoor garden too. Overly humid conditions are a prime contributor to its growth. One organic treatment that growers suggest is spraying the plant leaves with a solution of 1 part milk to 10 parts water at the first signs of mildew.

Common Disease Problems

When it comes to indoor growing, there are several types of diseases that can come into play, and here are general disease categories worth noting:

Fungal: Simply put, these involve a type of fungus that's trying to take over your plant's leaves and stems. Most often, this results in black spots, grayish mold or fuzz, rot at the base of the stems, or whitish powder coating leaves and stems. Sometimes, the plant seems fine and then suddenly wilts and dies within a short timeframe, which is an indication of root rot. Another fungal problem is "rust," which manifests as small, rust-colored bumps on the underside of leaves that eventually turn yellow.

Bacterial: When a detrimental bacteria affects your plant, the decline can happen fairly rapidly as the plant tries responding to the invader. The most common symptom of a bacterial problem is leaf spot, which can create round areas of dead cells on foliage, indicating infection. You might also see odd-looking bumps on stems, or abnormal growth on leaves and roots.

Viral: If a plant is suffering from a viral issue, it's most likely that you have an insect problem, since that's the most common way that plants get infected. Bugs feast on a diseased plant and then jump over to a healthy one and spread the disease when they begin their new meal. But viruses can also be spread by people, or even come from infected seeds. Plants with viral problems often appear stunted in some way, or misshapen. Leaves might roll up, or appear yellowish or white.

Abiotic: This is the term used when environmental factors cause problems rather than organisms like bacteria, fungus, or insects. Abiotic issues range from salt burn—caused by too much fertilizer in the soil—to sunburn from excessive light. I've sometimes seen frost damage occurring when a plant is put too close to a window during cold weather; the leaves might touch the chilled glass and then turn black as a result.

Fungal infections that select plants quite specifically are fairly rare in indoor gardens. The *Cercospora beticola* infection visible on these beet leaves is commonly known as "sugarbeet leaf spot" and can be combated only with harsh chemical pesticides that should not be used indoors. In most cases, the best action if you discover disease in your indoor garden is to discard the entire plant (and the soil it is in) before other plants are affected.

Prevention and Treatment

Reading about plant diseases can begin to feel disheartening, like browsing WebMD when you have a cold and walking away convinced you have scurvy. But don't worry—there are ways to prevent issues, and deal with them if they come up:

- Don't overwater: In the same way that mold can form from overwatering, diseases can find a hospitable environment in an overwatered plant.
- Don't overfertilize: Although you may think that more nutrients are better than fewer, there's danger in putting too much fertilizer into your plants. Specifically, the excess nitrogen can weaken a plant and affect its ability to resist diseases.
- Ventilate: I know it seems like I keep harping on airflow, but at the risk of constantly repeating myself, think about airflow. Ventilation is your friend.
- Space properly: When you crowd plants too close together (except for microgreens and shoots), problems can occur, so be sure to adhere to the spacing requirements for each plant based on seed company information or advice on specific crops found later in the book.
- Isolate: When dealing with a disease in a plant, move it away from your others, even if they're different types of plants. This helps to keep the disease contained to one area, and makes it easier to treat just one plant instead of several.
- Throw out: Sometimes, you put a great deal of effort into a project and it's just not working. If disease is the culprit, it's better to discard the plant and start fresh, because you don't want your other plants to be affected. It's also advisable to use the pot or tray for other purposes (pencil holder, perhaps, or an in-box for mail) because even if you thoroughly wash it, there's always a slight possibility that you didn't get all of it. I find it's better to be paranoid than to go through multiple rounds of fighting the same problem.

ATTITUDE

This may sound cheesy, or like the start of motivational speech, but a good attitude really does go a long way in your indoor growing efforts. When chatting with other avid gardeners, I'm often struck by the differences I see in how they approach their growing efforts. Some are so enthusiastic and joyful about their projects that they apologize for oversharing. They love to talk about what they're growing, they play and experiment and laugh off their failures because they embrace their successes so completely.

Others, however, are almost the polar opposite. They fret over their plants, get stressed about proper watering, and sometimes automatically assume that most of their efforts will falter. They're quick to throw out a struggling plant and then sigh miserably when talking about trying to find suitable replacements.

When I first started indoor edible gardening, I'd say my approach was definitely more Eeyore than Pooh, but over time, I gradually took on a more light-hearted attitude. After all, this is supposed to be fun, right? Sure, it can feel serious as you deal with aphids, yellowing leaves, lack of germination, and occasional mold incidents, but even with those challenges, it's still possible to see this whole venture as an experiment.

I once tried to grow mushrooms from inoculated logs in my basement, just to reset my attitude. Even though I managed to set up what I believed to be the perfect conditions, the project didn't work and I was stuck with some expensive firewood. Still, I took some good notes, realized my missteps, and I'm sure at some point, I'll give it another shot, or at least I'll get one of my much-more-experienced mycologist friends to grow some mushrooms for me. I won't stop doing crazy little projects, though, because yes, this really is supposed to be fun.

PART TWO

Microgreens, Shoots, Herbs, Wheatgrass, Sprouts, and Mushrooms

There are many types of edibles that are traditionally grown outdoors, but can be planted inside for fun—more on those in Part Three of the book—but there are also several kinds of "crops" that are ideally suited to an indoor growing environment. Specifically, microgreens, pea shoots, sunflower shoots, sprouted grains, and some herbs can thrive inside much better than they could fare in a garden.

These plants are often harvested at an early stage of a lifecycle, and they tend to be more fragile and delicate than what's growing outside in the garden. Sprouts, in particular, might do very poorly in outdoor conditions, even on a patio or deck, where sunlight early in the growing process might hinder germination.

For those who are new to indoor growing, the projects in this section are ideal as a starting point, and the quick seed-to-harvest timeframes mean that you won't be spending months waiting for vegetables to emerge. In fact, some microgreens can be harvested in less than a week, if factors are right.

These projects also help to determine if your indoor space is well suited for growing. Because of short timeframes, you'll be able to spot problems like airflow and overwatering more easily. For example, too much watering and stagnant air can create a mold situation in sunflower shoots or microgreens within just a few days, prompting the need to tweak your setup.

As with any indoor growing efforts, enjoy the process—especially when those pea shoots or fresh herbs can be thrown into dishes just moments after you harvest them.

REG. U.S
GROWN

MICROGREENS

Although some seed companies offer mixes designated as microgreens, there's no such thing as a "microgreen seed." They aren't grown using some special, almost magical seed that will grow a plant that's only about three inches in height. Instead, microgreens can be grown from nearly any seed, since they represent the first stage of growth of a plant.

Called cotyledons, these initial leaves of a seedling give way eventually to a plant's "true leaves," and from there the growth truly begins into vegetable, herb, or fruit. In other words, if you plant seeds in order to get microgreens and then change your mind or leave them for longer than intended, the plant will begin maturing and, most likely, get too large for the pot you've chosen. Most micros, by loose definition, are the cotyledon and first true leaves of a plant, although they can also be harvested at only the cotyledon stage.

When used as a garnish, microgreens add intense flavor and dense nutrients to savory dishes. This fried pork dish gets a big boost from a sprinkle of mustard microgreens.

Microgreens look similar to sprouted greens—and some online growing resources put them together in the same category—but unlike sprouts, which are grown in water, microgreens are grown in soil. They do best indoors, since trying to adjust planting density and moisture in outdoor conditions can be tricky.

In terms of arrival on the home garden scene, microgreens are the new kids on the block, but their popularity with chefs, small-scale farmers, and urban growers will likely propel microgreens past the trendy stage. Their cute size, mule-kick-level flavor, and nutritional clout make them a perfect addition to any indoor growing mix.

Although they're appearing more often on the menus at upscale restaurants, microgeens only started becoming popular in the last few years, and even the word itself is fresh. Mark Mathew Braunstein, author of *Sprout Garden* and *Radical Vegetarianism,* has noted that first use of the term "microgreens" was in 1998. By comparison, the first known use of the word "radish" appeared in the fifteenth century.

There's a reason microgreens are catching on quickly. According to a recent study in the *Journal of Agricultural and Food Chemistry,* microgreens can have up to forty times more nutrients than mature plants, ounce for ounce.

Their nutritional density depends on the type of microgreen, but all seem lush with nutrients. For example, red cabbage microgreens showed very high levels of vitamin C, vitamin K, and vitamin E. Considering how easy it would be to slip some micros into a kid's meal for an extra nutrient boost, keeping a small tray going in a kitchen garden makes sense.

Not just for garnishes, you can prepare a whole salad of microgreens for an amazing (and amazingly nutritious) taste treat. Radish and soy bean microgreens are being prepared here.

Talk about instant gratification. Most microgreens, including these peashoots, are ready to eat less than weeks after planting.

Most of all, though, there's the flavor. A single, slender beet microgreen only as long as a fingertip, for example, can taste like a fully grown beet. Mustard and radish microgreens are far spicier than many people might expect, and carrot microgreens carry the fresh, sweet flavor of just-harvested vegetables. They sometimes seem like the gum stolen by Violet in *Charlie and the Chocolate Factory*, when she tastes an entire dinner in a single stick. (Fortunately, unlike Violet's experience, there aren't any nasty side effects.) Also, when kept in glass containers in the refrigerator, micros can last for up to two weeks, and still maintain their punch.

For those who are just getting started with indoor growing, microgreens are an ideal initial project, and even for those who are experienced pros with kitchen gardens, the "crop" offers such endless variety that there's always something new and zesty to try. So, let's get growing.

Some seed companies have developed certain varieties that are best for growing microgreens, but in general, you shouldn't pay more for microgreen seeds since most seeds will grow into the micro stage.

Choosing Seeds

Although most seeds can grow into microgreens, there are some choices that make more sense than others. Melons or squash, for example, produce thick and chewy cotyledons that don't taste particularly tempting. Daikon radish or purple kohlrabi, though, are both particularly flavorful and provide pretty micros. Here are some guidelines for choosing well:

Personal taste: Those fond of strong, spicy flavors should gravitate to mustards, arugula, radishes, cress, and other zesty greens. If a milder taste is preferred, stick with options like chard, basil, cabbage, or carrot. Imagine the full flavor of a vegetable whittled down to a sliver, and that should determine your choice. When I forgot this rule, I ended up planting a whole tray of scallion micros that overpowered every dish I sprinkled them on, and caused onion breath for three days. Unless you hate your dentist or want to ruin a first date, you may want to make a wiser choice.

Germination time: Some micros mature rapidly, even within a few days, while

Mixes vs. Individual Varieties

Some gardeners and farmers enjoy creating a visual layering system, in which micros like beets, radish, and mustard create bands of different colors. Others might mix the seeds together before planting so the micros are somewhat pre-blended before harvest. Some seed companies sell mixes, which can be significantly less expensive than buying individual seeds and blending them. Another advantage to a pre-mixed package is that the varieties will mature at the same rate, making harvest much easier and ensuring a uniform "crop."

Blending several different types of seeds before planting allows you to harvest your mixed greens directly. Simply add some seeds that go well together, like beets, radish, and mustard, to a small jar and gently stir.

others might putter along and take ten days to a few weeks. Most people aren't trying to time micros according to menu planning or farmers' market selling, so germination time isn't especially important, unless you're creating a seed mix. In that case, it's usually a good idea to put fast-growing varieties with each other to prevent harvesting a tray of half-grown micros.

Color and appearance: Plenty of micros boast visual appeal, and planting a variety based on color can yield a tray that pops. Red-veined sorrel is gorgeous, almost cartoonish, in appearance, while red and golden beets sport brightly colored stems that seem almost like neon. For micros grown into the true leaves stage, it's fun to pick varieties with visual interest like garnet mustard, with a spray of red color against a green background, or mizuna, with its tiny, tree-like leaves.

Price: When choosing seed mixes or other microgreen varieties, keep in mind that anything designated as "microgreen seed" should be the same price as seeds that don't have that trendy title. If you pay more for beet microgreen seeds than you do for beet seeds from the same vendor, the price difference is probably going toward holiday bonuses for the seed company's marketing department.

Good Varieties for Indoor Growing

Nearly any microgreen seed variety is well geared for beginning growers, and it can be tough to limit an indoor garden to just a few. To get started, here are some of my favorites (see Resources section at the back of the book for seed purveyors):

- *Arugula:* Boasting purple stems, arugula is a nice addition to any mix that's heavy on green colors, and the spicy flavor is distinctive.

Arugula

- *'Red Giant' mustard:* Any variety of mustard is fun to throw into a micro blend because the flavors will really come through; with the Red Giant, the leaves have red veins throughout, making them visually appealing.

'Red Giant' Mustard

- *Beets:* So pretty as they're growing, with vibrant stems depending on whether you've planted red or golden beets. They take longer to mature, sometimes 3 weeks to nearly a month, so I tend to grow them separately rather than in a mix.

'Early Wonder Tall Top' Beet

- *Cress:* These can be very delicate and susceptible to mold if overwatered, but when cared for properly, they grow very quickly, sometimes within just a few days. They're easy to plant intensively, and have a fresh peppery flavor.

Cress (Cressida)

- *Komatsuna:* A Japanese spinach with a strong mustard flavor, the microgreen version mimics the vegetable's round, green leaves.

Komatsuna

- *'Ruby Red' chard:* With a mild, beet-like flavor, this variety also stands out for its reddish-pink stems, which look awfully pretty in a salad or sprinkled over eggs. Another great chard option is 'Bright Lights,' which combines gold, pink, orange, red, white, and purple stems. Think rainbow chard, but in a teeny tiny version.

'Ruby Red' Chard

- *'Red Russian' kale:* Personally, I love kale, so I tend to grow a lot of it during the year, both in micro and full-form versions. This variety has a nice pop of color thanks to a pinkish outline around the leaves.

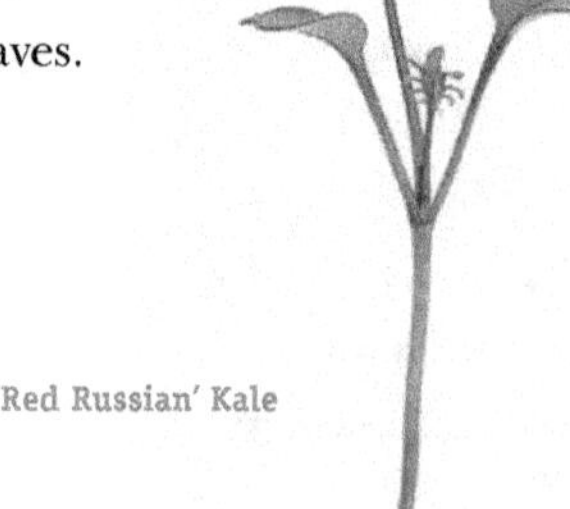

'Red Russian' Kale

- *'Dark Opal' basil:* Herbs are always a nice addition to a micro blend, and I like a strong basil flavor. This variety also boasts a purple leaf, which is a refreshing contrast to the dominant greens seen in most micros.

'Dark Opal' Basil

All the equipment you'll need for a large microgreens planting is assembled here.

Trays, Pots, and Other Containers

In addition to nutrient density, flavor, and the ability to impress dinner guests, microgreens are remarkably easy to grow in just about any type of pot or tray. Since they don't grow to maturity, they boast shallow root systems that make them ideal for planting in an array of containers.

Sometimes, you don't even need a tray: one summer, half-dazed from a day of planting, I spilled about a quarter cup of seeds on the passenger side of my Volkswagen Beetle convertible. Since the car is awash in mud, dirt, straw, twine, and other farm-related debris, I just wiped the seeds onto the floor mat and planned to vacuum them later, during my annual fit of vehicle cleaning. Because the car gets ample ventilation and sunshine from having the top down, and the floor mats are frequently wet from mud boots and random water bottles, the conditions were ideal for microgreens, and one morning I found a beautiful indoor mat of micro radishes, mizuna, and mustards.

Given my suspicion about the toxins that might be present in automotive mats and carpeting, my little crop went to waste, sadly. But the experience led me to use more shallow trays than I'd been employing, and to increase ventilation for my indoor efforts.

Although drainage is important for larger-scale growing, it's also fun to play around with fun growing-container options. Why not grow a coffee mug full of herbs?

An array of clever microgreen growing tactics exist, from putting a few seeds and a teaspoon of soil into bottlecaps, to utilizing old Pyrex baking dishes. But for an ideal system, I tend to prefer open-style seedling trays with drainage slots in the bottom. The slots keep the soil from collecting too much moisture, which can quickly lead to mold in a microgreen tray, even with adequate ventilation.

Also, when the microgreens reach a certain stage of growth, about three to four days before harvest, watering them from above can flatten the plants since they're somewhat delicate and have thin stems. Instead, they can be watered from the bottom (more on this later) thanks to the drainage slots.

You can use practically any leftover plastic container for growing microgreens. The best ones to use, though, are foodsafe containers that are designed for holding produce.

When choosing a pot or tray, keep soil usage in mind. Because of those roots, the micros don't need the type of soil depth you'd see with plant starts or even indoor herb gardens. Save soil by choosing a smaller container, and make harvest easier with a tray or pot that's shallow rather than deeper.

An open tray can be a boon during harvest, too. When I first started planting microgreens, I tried growing different varieties in a tray with separate sections, like you'd use for seed starting. While the sections are perfect for helping vegetables or herbs establish root balls and become hearty for transfer outdoors, it was a miserable choice for micros when it came to harvest. Normally, I cut micros with a scissors, but because each section was so separate from the others, I had to harvest with a tiny pair of embroidery scissors. While this was fun initially—my hands looked gigantic compared to those diminutive shears and miniscule plants—the whimsy wears off fast.

The shallow root systems grown when plants are at the ready-to-eat stage mean that even very shallow containers can be used as vessels for growing micros.

Loose soil that resists compaction is important, and prewatering the soil gives you a jumpstart on growing.

Soil Prep

Microgreens do best with very loose soil with good drainage, so I tend to use compost mixed with a little vermiculite. The most important part of soil prep is to add some water to the mix before planting, which helps to hold in moisture during the germination phase. For more on making Bossy E's Best Blend, go back and reread page 35.

When blending water and compost, go for a consistency that's like a crumbly brownie mix—then pick up a handful and squeeze. If a few drops of water come out, that's perfect. If there's a steady stream of water, it means you've made the mixture too wet, and you should add more dry mix.

It's not mandatory to premoisten the soil this way, and I've planted plenty of trays that did fine without it, but I've found that it can speed germination time by a few days if you use this method.

Planting and Care

First Steps

Make sure you start with a clean tray, pot, or other container, and add just a few inches of your soil mix, making sure to "fluff it up" if necessary.

Because the mix is moist, there's often a temptation to push the soil down as if making a mudpie, but this creates a soil compaction issue that can turn your micro tray into a hardened brick when it's put under light.

Here's the tricky part: seed generously. For those who are used to carefully dropping a single seed into a pot, it can take some time to overcome the psychological hurdle that microgreens present. But you need to seed heavily so that you can maximize your container's space, and also harvest more efficiently.

Granted, I'm guessing that you're not likely to become a professional microgreen grower, so harvest time is probably not a factor in your gardening strategy. But if you want to dress up a dish with a handful of micros, it will feel surprisingly time consuming to be clipping each one individually.

Here's an even more challenging part for many gardeners: don't cover the seeds with soil, vermiculite or anything else. If you do, then they tend to germinate unevenly, which isn't important if you're sowing seeds in a field, but is frustrating if your "field" is a small tray on your kitchen counter.

Prepare a blend of Bossy E's favorite soil (see page 35) and place a layer into your planting dish. If your soil seems too dense, just fluff it up a little.

Water very lightly, and then place a dish towel or empty tray over the top of the micro tray. This will help to keep the soil warm, and blocking the light for a few days helps the seeds to become healthier in general. You can peek inside if you want to see the magic—this isn't a soufflé—but be sure to replace the cover if the seeds haven't sprouted yet.

Once they show any sign of growth (about three to four days), remove the cover and water daily. Place under lights for at least six to eight hours per day.

Spread the seeds fairly densely. Don't cover the seeds with soil, vermiculite, or anything else. If you do, then they tend to germinate unevenly.

Lightly water the soil, taking care to avoid any pooling.

After a light watering, a dishtowel or other cover will help to retain heat and boost germination. Once they show any sign of growth (about three to four days), remove the cover and water daily.

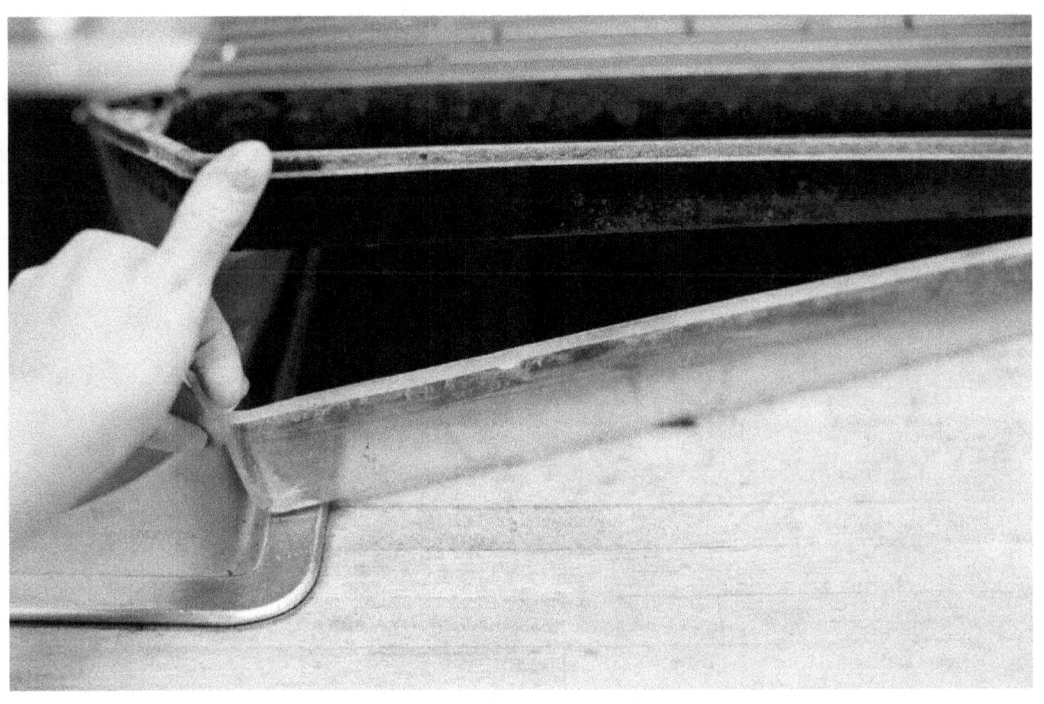

Tip: Once the greens have sprouted, do not water them from above. Instead, bottom water by setting the tray into a larger container and letting the growing medium soak up the water. Alternatively (but not as safe), water carefully at the root level or mist.

Maintaining Growth

Once they've established, microgreens don't require much care—that's one of the major benefits of growing them. But there's one important maintenance task that, if skipped, can put your micros in jeopardy.

The task is watering them properly. When they're just in the first stage of growth, before getting their true leaves, it's fine to water from above, but once they're looking very micro-like, it's crucial to "bottom water" them so the delicate stems and leaves don't get flattened.

Simply fill a kitchen sink, bathtub, even another empty tray, with about an inch of water and set the micro tray into it for a few minutes. The plant will take up the water it needs and hydrate the roots that way. This tactic is also useful if micros are looking droopy and need to perk up.

If you don't have a way to bottom water, then just water carefully at root level, or mist heavily instead of watering.

Troubleshooting

Some common problems and potential solutions for micros:

Moldy Clumps inside a Tray

This can be a result of improper airflow, overwatering, or too much humidity. If there are unaffected micros in the tray, lift out that section (throw out the moldy part) and relocate into a different tray, letting the soil dry out a little before you water again. Wait a few days before harvesting to see if mold develops on this section as well; if it does, discard and start over.

Tiny Threads of White around Seeds

Fortunately, this isn't an actual issue, it will just feel that way. This isn't mold—those little threads are called root hairs, and they're crucial for plant growth. They're very common for micros, and their purpose is to collect nutrients and moisture from the soil and deliver them to the entire plant. It's easy to mistake them for mold, but don't throw out the micros thinking that you've flubbed it—they're a sign that things are going right.

Yellow Micros that Look Sickly

If the micros are yellowish when you take off the top tray or dish towel, then you don't have a problem. They only appear that way because they need light to green up, and that should happen within a day or two at the most. If the micros are yellowing at another time, then they might be too far from their light source. Place them within 6 inches of whatever bulb you're using—unless it's a grow light that gives off heat (in which case: What are you doing using that? Are you trying to grow lizards?), don't worry about "burning" the micros, they should get a nice boost from the added photosynthesis.

Slow or No Germination

Most of the time, this happens because seeds are too old or because the tray isn't getting enough moisture. If it's the latter, simply water more often. If it's the former, you can do a germination test by putting a few seeds on a wet paper towel. They should start to germinate within two to four days, and if they don't, then get some fresh seed and give it another try.

Under good growing conditions, your microgreens should be ready to harvest in one to two weeks. Most types are at their tastiest when they are 1 to 2 inches tall and have spouted a second set of leaves.

Harvesting and Preservation

Getting Ready to Pick

Grab a handful and cut. Really, it's just that easy. In some cases, you'll see seeds that haven't germinated because others have blocked their light, so you can keep the tray going and see if you can get a second harvest from it. But in general, clear the tray and then start again.

Harvesting micros is easy work, and just takes a few moments with a scissors.

Storage Considerations

Although many microgreens are sold in plastic containers—at Bossy Acres, we sell them that way at farmers' markets because it's easier for transportation and cooling—the best way to keep them fresh is in glass containers. Pop them in a Mason jar or a Pyrex container with a lid, and they'll keep for a few weeks, sometimes even longer, in your refrigerator.

Store freshly harvested microgreens in a glass jar with a lid. Don't pack them in tightly.

In a sealed glass jar your microgreens will keep for at least a week if refrigerated. But you should always try to eat them when they are at their freshest.

Using Microgreens

The bad news is that long-term storage of microgreens isn't possible or realistic, unless you throw them in a pasta sauce that gets frozen or canned. But with the very short timeframe that comes with growing micros, keeping them long-term doesn't feel as important as it would for some crops.

The last bit of advice I have for micros: use them liberally. For many people (including myself), microgreens can spark creativity in terms of cooking and flavor combinations. Put them over salmon, chicken, tofu, or pork. Top a pizza with zesty arugula micros, or sprinkle some kale micros on a sandwich.

Just when scrambled eggs seem like the most boring dish on the planet, I throw a handful of Bright Lights chard micros on top and boom, I'm an amateur chef. Plus, who doesn't love a tiny forest of plants that grows within just a few weeks? Microgreens have become an indispensible part of my food landscape, and once you start growing them, I suspect they'll find a place on many of your plates, too.

Seared Ahi tuna with fruit salsa and microgreens

Cranberry sauce dressed with microgreens

Mixed salad with microgreens, mango, and black sesame seeds.

Hummus on a bed of microgreens with crisp bread.

PEA SHOOTS, SUNFLOWER SHOOTS, AND POPCORN SHOOTS

Sometime around the middle of February, it always seems to hit: the weariness of filling my shopping basket with fresh vegetables from California, Chile, Mexico, and even Peru or New Zealand.

No offense to the hardworking farmers across the U.S. and around the world, because I truly appreciate the opportunity to eat oranges during a snowstorm. But these products require, by necessity, lengthy shipping times that sap them of flavor and nutrition to some degree. Still, it's not easy to eat local when you live in a place that requires budgeting 20 minutes every morning for scraping the ice off your windshield. The only way it can be done in even a small way is to either grow what you can indoors, or tap into whatever canning and dehydrating you accomplished the summer before.

Since we tend to run out of our food preservation goodies by March in our house, it prompted us to begin experimenting with easy-to-grow options, and that led right to shoots.

Shoots make a delicious garnish on seafood or meat, or you can simply eat them by the bowlful. A pea shoot salad with lemon and olive oil is a sumptuous side dish.

Unlike sprouts—which are grown in water and require meticulous scheduling for rinsing and care to avoid bacterial issues—shoots are grown in soil, so it's a snap to be more flexible in terms of timing, resource usage, space, and other major factors. We began growing them just to see what would happen, and now our little farm is becoming a supplier of shoots for local restaurants—one of them has even dubbed a pea-shoot-laden veggie dish the "Bossy Burger." Who wouldn't want to eat that?

It's likely that you won't begin growing shoots on such a large scale that you have to sell them by the pound to local eateries, but there's definitely something addictive about seeing those shoots come up so quickly. The pea shoots have a soul-quenching crunch and a delicate flavor that tastes like spring, anytime. Sunflower shoots are nutty and succulent, with a texture that's surprisingly firm and holds up well in a sauté.

Popcorn shoots, our biggest experiment of all, are delightfully strange in their own right. They look a little like wheatgrass, but taste like very young sweet corn, then hit you with an aftertaste of corn stalk. I tend to blend all the shoots together to deal with that funky aftertaste, but some people have told me they now crave that flavor.

With these three options, shoots are only just a few weeks away from thriving under your own lights, so let's get started.

Shoots are sort of a cross between microgreens and sprouts. You plant them in growing medium, but you let them mature until they are roughly the same stage of growth as sprouts. Corn sprouts are seen here.

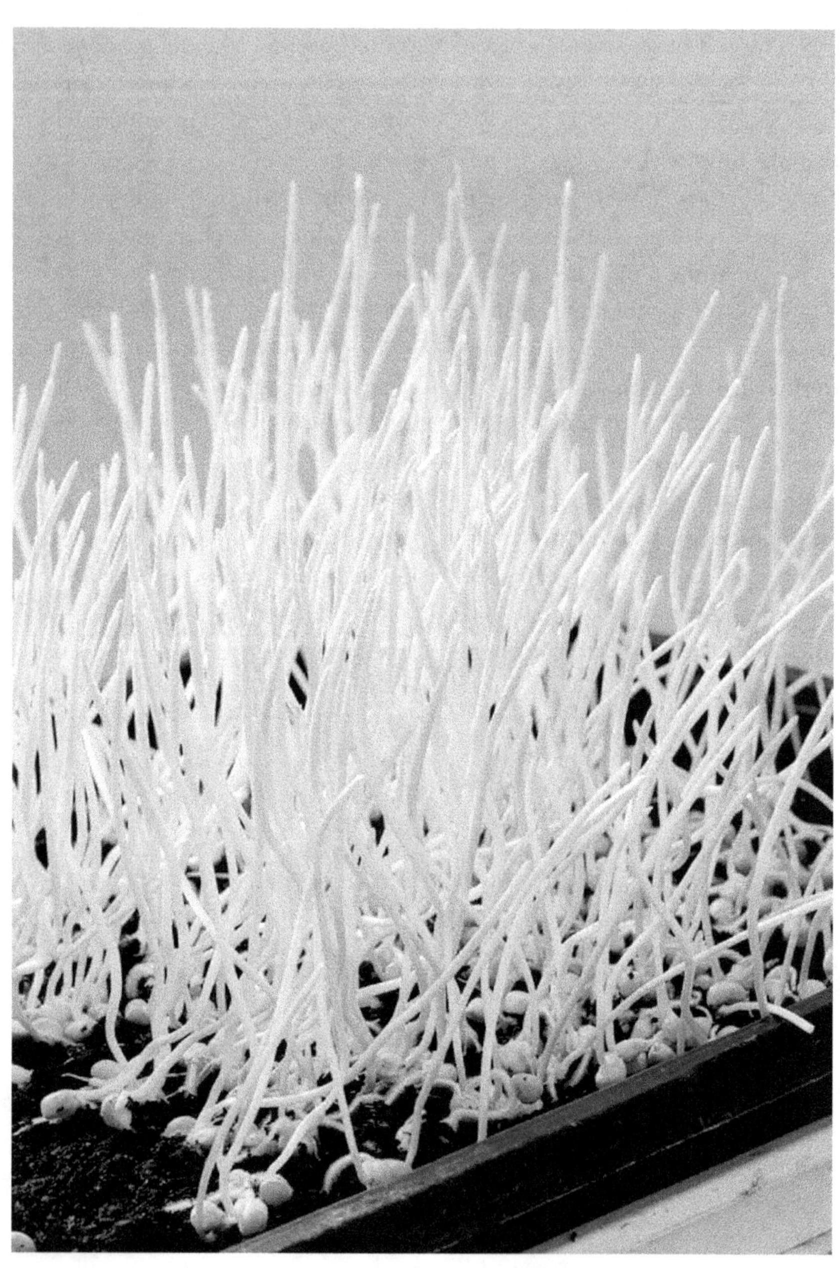

Good Options for Growing Shoots

In general, shoots are really just microgreens of the seeds you've chosen. So, if you were to let the peas, sunflowers, and popcorn grow into full maturity, you'd have those plants. But because you harvest them at such a young age, the flavors are more intense, and you can plant them much closer together in a flat tray. With shoots, variety doesn't tend to matter very much, although I've found better results with a specific type of pea seed. Here are some options:

- *'Dwarf Grey Sugar' peas:* After much experimentation, we now use only these, both for our farm and for home growing. They're developed to be shorter peas, so if you want to put some in your garden, you can get pea pods without having to do trellising. For indoor growing, I like them because they're hearty, easy to grow, and taste really amazing when you turn them into pesto. Nearly any other pea seed can be turned into shoots, however, so if you have some 'Sugar Snap' pea seed at home, that will work. I'd avoid varieties designed to be tall and robust, though, such as 'Oregon Giant.'

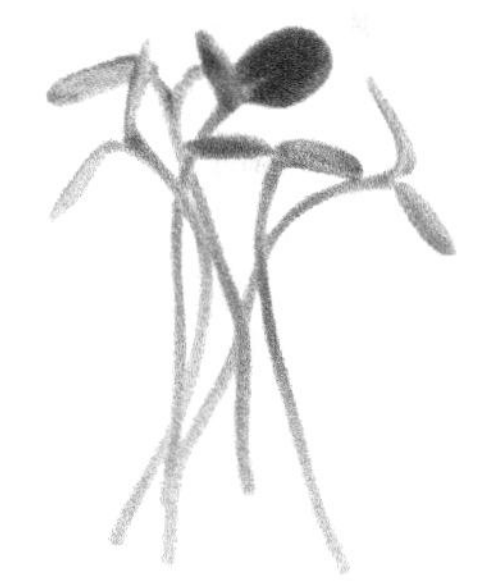

'Dwarf Grey Sugar' Pea shoots

- *Sunflower:* Although I include a list of resources at the end of the book, I'd planned to avoid mention of specific seed companies in the main body of the book because I don't want to seem biased. But here I'm going to break my own rule, because there's one company that provides excellent sunflower seeds for shoots, and they're even organic. Johnny's Selected Seeds, a company out of Maine, offers a sunflower seed variety that's highly dependable and very hearty. When I've tried other options, it's been disappointing, especially when I've played around with growing from sunflower seeds that are usually meant for bird feeders (I mentioned gardening is an adventure, right?). Stick with seeds meant for human consumption, and give Johnny's a try (See Resources, page 221).

Sunflower shoots

- *Popcorn:* On a whim, we wondered if we could buy organic popcorn from the co-op, sprout it, and then plant it and eat it as shoots. As it turns out, the answer is yes. So, you don't need to buy "seed" from anywhere as long as you have access to popcorn kernels that aren't processed, coated in oil, or salted in any way. Popcorn differs from corn kernels because popcorn is derived from specific strains of corn that were cultivated for the purpose. That means you might be able to sprout corn and get the same effect, but popcorn is more reliable if you're trying to grow shoots.

Popcorn shoots

- *Nasturtium:* One the most popular edible flowers, nasturtiums also make delicious shoots. As when planting in the garden, nasturtiums can be a little slow to sprout. Try soaking the seeds in water for an hour or longer before spreading them in the media.

Nasturtium shoots

When planted in a shallow tray, shoots quickly develop a thickly knit root mass. It isn't edible, but it makes great compost.

Trays, Pots, and Other Containers

Much like other types of microgreens, I tend to prefer open-style seedling trays with minimal depth and drainage slots in the bottom. The slots keep the soil from collecting too much moisture, which can quickly lead to mold in a shoots tray, even with adequate ventilation. That's because the seeds are sown so close to each other that without drainage, root rot can become an issue within just twenty-four hours of planting.

When choosing a pot or tray, keep soil usage in mind. Because of those roots, the shoots don't need the type of soil depth you'd see with plant starts or even indoor herb gardens. Save soil by choosing a smaller container, and make harvest easier with a tray or pot that's shallow rather than deeper.

Even though peas, sunflowers, and corn require plenty of space when it comes to root depth, when planted as shoots, a very curious thing happens: the roots begin to curl up into each other, creating a thick mat in the case of pea shoots, and turning your tray into a solid block. I tend to use shallow trays just for this reason, because composting the soil after harvest is easily done, like throwing a very small carpet onto the compost pile. Bonus for homesteaders: chickens *love* the leftover stems and seeds from shoots trays.

So, you use minimal soil, get maximum use from your tray, and maybe even make your chickens happy.

Prep Work

For shoots, I find that a pure compost mix (see Resources in the back of the book if you don't have a greenhouse near you) tends to work very well, as long as it's fairly "fluffy" in consistency. If all you have is indoor potting soil, lighten it up by adding vermiculite to the soil.

The most important part of soil prep is to add some water to the mix before planting, which helps to hold in moisture during the germination phase.

When blending water and compost, go for a consistency that's like a crumbly brownie mix—then pick up a handful and squeeze. If a few drops of water come out, that's perfect. If there's a steady stream of water, it means you've made the mixture too wet, and you should add more dry mix.

It's not mandatory to premoisten the soil this way, and I've planted plenty of trays that did fine without it, but I've found that it can speed germination time by a few days if you use this method.

For seed prep, there's a simple way to speed germination time: just soak the seeds for about twenty-four hours before planting. In some cases, especially when the house feels on the colder side, I soak them for a day or two longer so that they begin to sprout before I plant them. This can reduce germination by up to a week in some cases.

These sunflower seeds have just begun to sprout. Soaking the seeds in water for a day before planting them will speed up the shoots.

But be very careful about soaking during hot weather and for too much longer than about seventy-two hours maximum, because once they pass the stage where they're sprouting, they'll start to deteriorate and can't be planted. The worst part of forgetting to plant or putting it off for too long is that rotting, wet shoots seeds give off a stench that will permeate the house. Seriously, it's one of the worst stinks that you can imagine, like fungus-crusted toejam inside of wet, dirty socks. Just make it a point never to find out if I'm characterizing that aroma accurately.

Planting and Care

First steps

Make sure you start with a clean tray, pot, or other container, and add just a few inches of your soil mix, making sure to "fluff it up" if necessary. Because the mix is moist, there's often a temptation to push the soil down, but this creates a compaction issue that can turn your shoots tray into a hardened brick when it's put under light.

Another consideration when spreading soil is to take a moment to create a level surface, especially along the sides. Unfortunately, it's easy to let the soil build up on the sides slightly and come to a depression in the middle, but this inadvertent valley-like tray will cause unevenness in your water distribution, allowing some seeds to sit in water for too long while others dry out.

Once your soil mix is ready, seed generously. For shoots, this means you'll be creating a seed bed where the seeds look far too close together, but aren't overlapping. There's no need to poke holes in the soil mix and place seeds inside, they can sit on top of the soil and grow perfectly well that way.

Keep in mind that each seed will grow a shoot vertically, so it's fine if they're all just a few fractions of an inch from each other, but you don't want

Spread plenty of seeds onto your compost mix.

them competing for the exact same tiny stretch of soil.

If you do happen to sow them thicker and they're touching one another in parts, that's fine as well, just know that you might get less germination than expected. The good news is that these non-germinating seeds tend to get a second chance after your first harvest.

Water very lightly, and then place an empty black tray over the top of the micro tray. This will help to keep the soil warm, and blocking the light for a few days helps the seeds to become healthier in general. You can peek inside if you want to see the magic, but be sure to replace the cover if the seeds haven't sprouted yet.

Once they show any sign of growth (about three to four days), remove the cover and water daily. Place under lights for at least eight hours per day. You can give them a blend of artificial light and sunlight if you're in a season or a geographic area where the sun is strong enough, but keep in mind that the shoots will bend toward the light, so rotate the tray daily if necessary. Otherwise, place the tray directly under your growing lights, about 6 inches from the tops of the plants.

Do not cover the shoot seeds with planting medium. Make sure they have moisture and warmth and they'll begin shooting in a couple of days.

Pea shoots take around two weeks to mature for eating. A) Newly planted; B) 3 days; C) One week; D) Two weeks

Maintaining Growth

Once they've established, shoots don't require much care, which is a plus. But much like microgreens, they benefit greatly from a "bottom watering" strategy.

Simply fill a kitchen sink, bathtub, even another empty tray, with about an inch of water and set the shoots tray into it for a few minutes. The plant will take up the water it needs and hydrate the roots that way. This tactic is also useful if shoots are looking droopy and need to perk up.

If you don't have a way to bottom water, then just water carefully at root level, or mist heavily instead of watering.

Watering shoots from beneath is a good way to hydrate the roots without flattening the tender stalks.

When it's particularly humid in the house, (summertime in most cases) consider planting and replanting shoots only after the weather has cooled off. At Bossy Acres, we've tried to grow shoots year-round, and I've attempted the same tactic at home, but there are definitely better seasons than others when it comes to successful growing. Spring and fall are ideal. With heat mats, winter brings slower growth but still plenty of tasty shoots. Summer, however, is brutal for shoots even in a house with central air conditioning. Unless you love playing around with tweaking elements constantly—airflow, more watering, less watering, bottom watering, misting, more airflow, different placement, etc.—I'd suggest saving shoot growing for more temperate seasons rather than summer.

Shoots grow best in the spring and fall, but if you use a heat mat or another suitable heat source you can grow them successfully in winter too. Summer, with its heat and humidity, is a less-than-perfect environment for growing shoots indoors (but that's usually okay, because summer is a great time for growing edibles outdoors).

Here are some other tactics for keeping your shoots on track:

- Continue watering and providing light to the shoots tray after a first harvest. Many times, some seeds germinate later or are delayed because they're under other seeds. For pea shoots especially, you can get two to three more harvests because of this. These subsequent harvests won't be as abundant as the first ones, but they're enough to be worth the effort.

- If the air in your house seems especially dry, mist the plants when they're in an early stage of growth and then put a clear tray on top. These are available at any garden store, and they help to let in light but lock in moisture. I find these invaluable in the winter, especially when the shoots are just out of the germination stage, but not established enough yet. Alternately, you can also use plastic wrap, but just be sure that the shoots aren't grown enough to bump against the top of the wrap, which can impede growth.

- Another good tactic when the air is dry is to mist the plants more often during the day if they seem to be struggling. Be aware that this strategy could cause browning if the plants are close to an artificial light source, so raise the light or lower the plants by 6 inches and mist heavily if this happens.

Provide a little drainage by placing small rocks in the bottom of your planting vessel prior to adding the dirt.

Use a shallow to medium depth container for planting pea shoots.

Plant shoot seeds densely. Often, a second crop will pop up from the original seed planting after you harvest the first batch.

Troubleshooting Shoots

Some common problems and potential solutions for shoots:

No Germination, Even after a Few Days
Shoots tend to germinate quickly, so this would be a major issue. Most likely, it's related to the temperature of the soil. Putting a cover over the tray tends to keep the moisture and warmth inside, but sometimes you need an extra boost, so consider setting the tray on a heat mat (see page 95), which are available at any garden store. These rectangular mats raise the temperature slightly, just enough for the seeds to feel cozy, but not enough to damage them or to scorch your counter. You can leave it plugged in for days if necessary. If it's been a week and you're still not seeing germination, check the density of your soil mix and see if it's too hardened—compaction will often prevent the seeds from establishing.

Moldy Clumps inside a Tray
Moldy clumps can be a result of improper airflow, overwatering, or too much humidity. If there are unaffected shoots in the tray, lift out that section (throw out the moldy part) and relocate into a different tray, letting the soil dry out a little before you water again. Wait a few days before harvesting to see if mold develops on this section as well;

if it does, discard and start over. If the problem tends to be too much moisture from the start, which can happen during humid months, sow the seeds into dry soil instead of pre-wetting the soil mix, and do a thorough watering before covering the tray during the germination process.

Tops of the Shoots Are Browning or Turning Dark
You have them too close to the light source, so you're essentially cooking them in the tray. Move them away from the light by another 6 inches, clip off the browned tips, and hopefully the remainder will thrive.

Shoots Are Yellowing or Looking Droopy
Usually, yellowing means overwatering, so let your soil dry out a little. By contrast, droopy shoots are often caused by underwatering, or by too much humidity. In that case, bottom water the shoots in cold water and see if they perk up after about ten to fifteen minutes. Also, adjust your fans so that shoots are getting some airflow to disperse stagnant, humid air and increase circulation. Keep in mind that plants "breathe," and they need some airflow to keep oxygen levels high. If your efforts aren't successful and the shoots remain droopy, you may just want to harvest and eat—they'll still be tasty and nutritious, just a bit less crisp.

Just like microgreens, shoots do best stored in glass, and can last for weeks in the fridge this way. Pea shoots, though delicate, are remarkably long lasting and keep their crunch up until the end. Sunflower shoots are even tougher, and I've kept some for three weeks in the fridge without any discernable change in flavor. Popcorn shoots, though, tend to last for a shorter time and when kept for longer, that odd aftertaste gets stronger. So for those, I would harvest and eat the same day.

Shoots and microgreens packaged for sale will last quite awhile in the refrigerator.

Harvesting and Preservation

Getting Ready to Pick

For each variety of shoots, there is an ideal time for harvest:

- Pea shoots: These will grow long and look unruly, and I tend to harvest them when they're about 8 to 10 inches. If you want sweeter and more uniform shoots, harvest at around 4 inches when they're just beginning to unfurl their leaves. If you want a super abundant harvest, and a less pea-sweet taste, let them go until 12 inches. Longer than that, though, and they start to get too long and heavy for the tray, so they start flattening. Also, the taller they get, the more woody the flavor.

Pea shoots make a tasty and visually appealing garnish for most seafoods, including these seared scallops.

You can harvest pea shoots at any stage, but they tend to be best at 8 to 10 inches, before they get unruly. Younger pea shoots, like the ones seen here are just a few inches tall, but they can taste sweeter and have a more uniform size.

- Sunflower shoots: These taste best when you get them before the sunflowers develop their first true leaves. At the shoot stage, you'll have just two petals that are nicely crunchy. When the first true leaves begin sprouting, they come up between these petals and have a scratchy texture that I don't enjoy even though they're perfectly edible. If you let the shoots go for too long and the leaves start coming up, you can still enjoy the shoots-only taste and look by plucking off the true leaves and discarding them. In terms of what to harvest, I clip all the way down to the soil, because the stems are just as tasty as the leaves.

- Popcorn shoots: These are best at about 6 inches, and be sure to include some of the white-and-pink bottoms, where the most intense flavor resides. Once the shoots get taller, they're fun to have in the windowsill because they look so vibrant, but the taste becomes more and more grassy as they grow. At about 10 inches, the shoots have all the flavor and appeal of fresh lawn clippings.

Pea shoots can be a chief ingredient in a fresh green salad, with the strong flavor needed to stand up to savory meat like the ham hock above.

HERBS

One of the most satisfying projects for any kitchen gardener is an herb pot, brimming over with favorites like sage or cilantro, or ripe with a medley of different mints.

I've seen some great combinations put together—like creating a "pasta sauce herb garden" with oregano, thyme, and basil—and because most herbs thrive from frequent harvest, they're perfect for a kitchen space since you can just snip what you need for a particular dish.

For my kitchen space, I like to put herbs in separate pots so that I can isolate them in case of insect issues or mold problems. But I often create combinations when giving herb pots as gifts, and I always love the aromas that blend as a result of letting them tangle up together.

A windowsill herb garden is a welcome addition to any kitchen. This one, with its matching porcelain pots, features marjoram, rosemary, and lemon balm.

For a very small investment you can turn a sunny windowsill into a mini herb farm. One great thing about growing herbs is that you don't need much at one time, so a few mature plants can keep you well supplied with herbs.

In general, many herbs are well-geared toward indoor growing, and several of the gardeners I know repot their outdoor garden herbs as the weather here gets crisp, so that they can extend the growing season indoors.

Some herbs, such as rosemary, oregano, thyme, and sage, propagate well if you take a cutting from an existing outdoor or indoor plant and prepare it for growth inside. If that's your strategy, simply cut a 4-inch section (measured from the tip of the stem/ leaf toward the soil) and strip off about an inch or so of the lower leaves. Put the stem into a potting mix, such as vermiculite, and keep the mix somewhat moist as the plant establishes.

These plants like humidity, so cover with clear plastic or glass—letting light in, but trapping moisture—but don't let them get too hot from direct sunlight. Also, remove their covers occasionally or put them on a porch or "transitional" space to give them some air.

This technique also works well for transplants purchased at a greenhouse, which should already be "hardened" to temperature variations. In my experience, there are times when I just can't seem to grow certain herbs from seed (I'm looking at you, basil) and I need the jumpstart that a transplant can provide. When I began my indoor growing adventures, I relied on transplants almost entirely because I appreciated being able to skip that first big leap in germination. These days, however, I actually enjoy the planting process, and tend to choose herbs that thrive best in my kitchen.

So, for this section, we'll take a closer look at how to go from seed to harvest, so you can get a feel for growing herbs entirely indoors. If you do go the transplant or herb-cutting route, though, much of the information still applies, particularly when it comes to issues like soil drainage and temperatures.

Some herbs can be started from seed indoors; others can be propagated from cuttings you take from your outdoor plants.

Good Varieties for Indoor Growing

Although many herbs do beautifully in an indoor growth space, some varieties can be surprisingly fickle if you're trying to grow them from seed. Here are some options, broken down by level of difficulty:

Easy Like a Sunday Morning

- *Peppermint and spearmint:* Hearty and wide-ranging, mint likes to invade the territory of other plants, so once you've got it, stay on top of harvesting it. If you want a strong mint taste without growing a bunch of it, opt for peppermint, since it has a more intense flavor.

- *Lemongrass:* You don't even plant this one from seed; just buy a stalk of lemongrass from a grocery store or farmers' market, trim the top, and put the stalk in a few inches of water. The stalk will produce roots on its own and dozens of new shoots, and you can harvest from these.

- *Vietnamese coriander:* This variety is considered easier to grow than other varieties of coriander, and it has just as much flavor. Also, it's quite hearty and can last for months.

Takes Effort, but Generally Doable

- *Parsley:* Usually fairly easy to grow, but germination can be hit and miss. Usually, you'll begin to see growth about two weeks after planting, and it tends to grow slower than other herbs in general.

- *Oregano:* The trick with oregano is giving the plant enough light every day; it may require placing the pot under a separate bulb that's on for a few hours more than the other herbs. Usually, about eight hours of light is best.

- *Thyme:* This herb also requires more light, so I often put oregano and thyme in the same space or place them next to each other in a south-facing window.

- *Rosemary:* I've found that my best indoor rosemary comes from cuttings off rosemary in my garden, but it's also somewhat easy to grow by seed. Watch out for overwatering, since rosemary tends to prefer drier soil, and be sure to choose a variety that does well with indoor growing, like 'Blue Spire.'

- *Chervil:* Fairly uncommon, but quite delicious, chervil is related to parsley and has a subtle flavor. The herb does well in low-light areas, making it a nice choice for kitchen corners and out-of-the-way spots, but keep in mind that it doesn't do well when temperatures begin to rise beyond 70 degrees, so gauge your house's temp before planting.

More Challenging

- *Basil:* It's so ubiquitous in cooking, you'd think basil would be a snap to grow in your kitchen garden. But no. Notoriously difficult to grow indoors from seed, basil tends to work best as a plant start from a greenhouse. Also, those lush Italian basil leaves may not be as wide and pretty as you find in a garden. Instead, I lean toward varieties with smaller leaves like 'Dark Opal' or Thai basil.

- *Cilantro:* Here's another one that grows remarkably well outside but requires a higher level of care indoors. First of all, it doesn't transplant well, so it needs to be grown from seeds or starter plants. Also, it requires plenty of drainage and yet needs more nutrients, making it tough to keep the soil nourished. It tends to do fine once it's established, but until then, plan on giving the herb fertilizer biweekly, which will be twice as much as your other herbs. Also, water only when the soil seems very dry.

- *Sage:* It isn't too difficult to get sage started indoors, but it's prone to death by overwatering. There have been many times where I see those tough leaves and think the plant looks dry, and then I end up killing it because it's already well watered. Also, many experts advise waiting a long time before harvesting while the plant gets established—up to a year in some cases. For me, the space in my kitchen growing area is too limited to nurse a plant that takes months before I can use it, but I do like to have a small pot going because the herb dries so well after harvest.

Soil Prep

Herbs are quite finicky when it comes to drainage. Common gardener wisdom is that they "don't like wet feet," which means that if their roots get too soggy, rot will result. Every plant type covered in this book (except sprouts) relies on proper drainage to some degree, but for herbs, it's particularly crucial because they tend to like a more humid environment, making them susceptible to root rot.

Simply using a pot with holes in the bottom isn't enough, and if you buy a standard type of pot with a dish that catches water, you'll be in even more trouble. This often leads to an herb sitting in water, which is almost always a terrible situation for the plant.

There are a number of strategies that can be helpful for increasing drainage. Some gardeners use a system designed for growing cactus, because these specialty mixes are designed to drain quickly, but I find that simply mixing sand and vermiculite (in a one-to-four parts ratio) together tends to make a happy blend.

If you are planting herbs from seed, make sure the soil is not too densely packed. If need be, cultivate it by loosening the soil with your fingers.

If you're transplanting from outside, do as much as you can to remove the existing garden soil by gently shaking or tapping the roots. You won't be able to eliminate all of the soil, but if you can get most of it, you'll significantly reduce your expose to garden pests and diseases.

Whatever you use, a good strategy to prevent compaction is to cultivate within the pot every month or so. You can simply take a fork and gently loosen the soil within the container, taking care to stay mostly on the periphery so you don't damage the roots.

Trays, Pots, and Other Containers

At the risk of harping too much on drainage, I'm going to emphasize the importance of drainage again. I can even put it in italics if it helps: *drainage.* Herbs just don't do well at all in any situation where they're sitting in water, so choose a container or pot that allows for ample flow.

Sure, you can try growing cilantro in your middle school lunchbox or parsley in that repurposed desk drawer or whatever other funky container appeals to you, but if you want to keep the herbs going for a nice long time, drill some holes and maybe even throw some pebbles in the bottom. Your herbs will thank you.

Beyond that, any material works, but I tend to shy away from terra cotta pots because they make the herbs dry out faster, and that throws off my estimation of how much watering they need.

Because of limited space, I gravitate toward smaller pots, but if the herbs begin to spread too far over the edges, or I want to encourage them to get bigger, I'll repot into a larger container.

Planting and Care

First Steps

Get your container and soil mix ready (see pages 27 to 35), and give the mix some water so it's slightly damp. This will keep your seeds from shifting when you first water them.

Sow the seeds about one to three times deeper than the size of the seed. This is a general rule, and what it usually means for me is that if it's a teensy little seed, I'll barely press it into the soil, and then I'll cover it with just a sprinkling of vermiculite. If the seeds are larger, I might press about half an inch and then cover it.

Water lightly, and then cover the pot or container with plastic kitchen wrap. This will keep the soil mix and seed warm, to encourage germination. Put the pot or container in a sunny area or under a light, and when the seedlings emerge, remove the plastic wrap.

Maintaining Growth

Some herbs require specialized care, but in general, most can benefit from these tips for keeping herbs going strong:

- Fertilize every 10 days or so with diluted fish fertilizer, found at any garden store. In a pinch, I've also soaked seaweed in hot water for a few hours, let it cool, and then sprayed that on the plants. But for this to be an "in a pinch" tactic,

Herb seeds don't need to be planted too deep, just press them gently into the soil with your finger.

you'd have to be one of those people who happens to have dried seaweed in the cupboard.

- Herbs like humidity, but it's not always easy to tweak this condition, especially in the winter. One good tactic is to create a tray of small rocks or pebbles and fill the tray with water, leaving about ¼ inch of the top dry. Put the pots on top of the trays—making sure they don't touch the water—and the evaporation process will help to keep the air at a nice humidity level.

- Give herbs a regular "bath" by misting every few days. Not only does this help to keep the hydrated, but it also cuts down on insect issues since weakened plants are more susceptible to pests like aphids and spider mites.

- Water from the base of the herb, not the leaves. This will help the plant get hydrated, without subjecting it to "flattening out" from too much water hitting the leaves.

Fish fertilizer is available from any garden store, and when diluted, can provide a nice boost for any type of plant.

Troubleshooting Herbs

Some common problems and potential solutions for herbs:

Slow Growth or Limited Germination

Potentially, this could be a light issue. Herbs need at least five hours of light per day to stay healthy, and full-on sunshine (provided the area isn't too hot) is ideal. But in the winter, even a south-facing window might not be enough. If you're seeing sluggish growth, try extending the time that the herbs are under light, up to fourteen hours if necessary.

Brown Patches or Withered-Looking Leaves

If your herbs are under a light source, they may be too close to the bulb. Basically, you're burning them. Herbs should be at least 6 to 8 inches away from the light source, and that distance is measured from bulb to the top of the plant.

Whitish Fuzz on Soil

This might be natural seed germination, but it could also be mold. Check that you're not overwatering—if you put your finger into the soil mix and feel moisture immediately, then this could be the issue. Let the plant "dry out" and isolate it from the other plants in the meantime. Remove the moldy areas, but be aware that you may need to start over with this one.

Stems Seem Soft or Mushy

This may be another incidence of overwatering. Stems tend to feel too soft when root rot is occurring. Another big indication of problems is a foul smell mixed in with the pleasant herb scents.

Bug Infestation in Progress

It's so disheartening to lean over a pot of herbs, ready to snip off a few selections for dinner, and see that something else is ahead of you in the buffet line. If this happens, isolate the plant and try a soap spray—this can be a mix of mild liquid soap (like Dr. Bronner's) and water. Spray in the evening, since application when the plant is in full sunlight can cause drying.

Some herbs, like sage, are prone to browning or yellowing of the leaves. Often, it is caused by over-exposure to heat.

Harvesting and Preservation

Getting Ready to Pick

Each herb is harvested in its own way, but in general, go for the "older" leaves that are full. Look for new growth, usually near the center of the plant, and avoid clipping near that area since you don't want to shorten the lifespan of the herb.

If a plant begins to flower, snap off the flowering part as soon as you can to prolong the herb's timeframe—like many plants, herbs begin flowering as a signal that they're done growing (it's a process called "bolting"). By removing the flowers, you can essentially trick the plant into sticking around for longer.

When harvesting, keep in mind that stems tend to have abundant flavor as well. For example, cilantro stems are just as intensely flavored as the leaves.

CORRECT: Cut older, mature leaves on the outer area of the plant.

INCORRECT: Do not harvest the new, inner growth of the herb plant.

Herbs can be bundled and dried hanging upside-down right in your kitchen.

Storage Considerations

Due to a recent homesteading kick, I've been experimenting with various ways to preserve just about everything, from canned cabbage to dehydrated celery. Compared to trying to preserve artichokes, herbs are a snap.

There are so many ways to make sure that your herbs can last for months. The quickest method is through drying—simple create a bundle, strip off about an inch of leaves to expose only stems, tie with twine or a rubber band, and hang up in a cool, dry area. There's a section of my basement that smells pretty amazing at this point, thanks to multiple herb bundles. The advantage of drying is that you can leave the bundles hanging for quite a while, or just crumble them when they're completely dry and put them into glass jars.

Another storage option is preservation in olive oil. Make sure the glass jar is very dry, and then fill it with herbs like basil, thyme, and oregano, as well as other ingredients like garlic. Fill the jar with olive oil, making sure the oil completely covers the herbs, and in about six weeks, the oil will be infused with flavor. After that, you can strain out the herbs and drizzle the new creation over whatever you like.

Similarly, you can finely chop herbs, put them in a glass jar, and cover completely with honey. In six weeks, the flavor will infuse the honey, and in this case, I don't try to strain out the herbs.

This blend can be used in place of jam on toast, or some people simply eat a spoonful when they're feeling energy depleted, especially if more medicinal herbs are used.

Overall, herbs are a stellar addition to any kitchen garden, and incorporating even just a few favorites can help boost the flavors of your dishes. At this point, I'm irritatingly snobby when it comes to "fresh" herbs that I see at the grocery store, since they look so tired and depleted. Knowing that my herbs are harvested only about ten minutes before I enjoy them makes me feel spoiled, especially in the winter when that level of freshness would be so difficult to achieve otherwise.

You have to make a significant commitment of indoor real estate to grow enough basil to keep your kitchen stocked in pesto. But if you love fresh pesto you'll find the space.

Herbs are built for garnishing; and not parsley alone. A sprig of thyme gives life to any egg dish, and also blends with this savory carrot soup.

WHEATGRASS & PET GRASS

Smoothies and juice are the most common forms in which to consume wheatgrass, although many who believe in its health benefits simply blend it up and take a wheatgrass shot like the one above.

Before I began growing wheatgrass myself, I considered the plant to be something of a 1970s throwback, making me think of hemp burgers, bell bottoms, and paisley. Since I've seen all three of those on a recent shopping trip through Target, maybe it's safe to say that retro is the future.

For those of us who've become fans of wheatgrass, it's very fortunate that it's not relegated to the hippie era, or even to the 1980s-esque power generation of juicing and shoulder pads. Instead, wheatgrass seems to hang on through the decades, and that's for good reason.

All kinds of claims have been made trumpeting wheatgrass' benefits, from curing cancer to prolonging a youthful glow without plastic surgery. But despite the hyperbole, some of the more impressive claims actually have scientific backing. According to the Mayo Clinic, a leading healthcare and research institution, wheatgrass is nutrient dense, and provides a concentrated amount of iron, calcium, magnesium, amino acids, chlorophyll, and vitamins A, C, and E. The Mayo notes that there are no significant research studies to support health claims, but does acknowledge anecdotal evidence that wheatgrass can boost immunity, rid your body of waste, and kill harmful bacteria in your digestive system.

In terms of taste, that's another matter. Not surprisingly, I find it strongly grassy, and feel a bit like a goat whenever I have a wheatgrass shot, but I can't deny that I feel an energy jolt about ten minutes later. Also, if you're juicing or making green smoothies, wheatgrass is incredibly easy to add into the mix without making the whole concoction taste like you're gnawing on sod.

Best of all, it's simple to grow. Before we get into the specifics, I also included pet grass in this section because you can grow it using the same tactics, and it's purported to have the same type of benefits for pets that wheatgrass does for humans. I've heard from several gardeners who grow pet grass rather than catnip because it's a good digestive aid that doesn't make their cats race around the house looking for trouble. Pet grass also makes for nice critter control if you put some in front of other plants—cats will nibble on the grass and hopefully lose interest in the other options.

Cat grass is good for your pet's digestive system, especially if your cat is an indoors-only pet. If you place the plants strategically, you may be able to distract the cat from nibbling on the other edibles you're growing.

Good Varieties for Indoor Growing

Wheatgrass seeds are also known as wheat berries or hard winter wheat seed. Some of these types of seeds are sold as cover crops for farmers and may be pretreated with pesticides, so please source carefully. Check out the Resources page in the back of the book for options (I'm only including reputable purveyors with plenty of organic and sustainable choices), and if you're

A close-up shot of organic wheatgrass seed.

buying locally, you can sometimes find good wheatgrass seeds at co-ops and health food stores, or garden stores that sell organic seeds.

Pet grass, also called cat grass or catgrass, is a cereal grass as well. Although it may be the same as wheatgrass, it could also be grown from buck-oat grass seeds. They provide cats with added roughage in their diets and help to remove hairballs.

In other words, pet grass and wheatgrass can be the same thing, but it's often nice to grow two different types in order to keep a feline from seeing your entire wheatgrass tray as her domain.

Pet grass (also called cat grass) can be grown using the same seed as wheatgrass, or it may be grown with buck oat grass seed.

This may not be the safest container, but there is no reason you can't grow wheatgrass in recyclable cans.

Trays, Pots, and Other Containers

Since wheatgrass and pet grass grow very evenly, I like to use a flat tray with drainage holes in the bottom, to maximize the space. But you can also grow on a smaller scale by repurposing the type of clear plastic pint containers used for selling berries, for example.

These containers are ideal for this purpose because they already have holes in the bottom, can be easily shifted to different spaces, and the clear plastic lets you see the roots growing inside—a surefire way to get kids more interested in gardening, but also quite cool for adults. That might be my garden geek side talking, though.

Wheatgrass grows very densely and can be planted in shallow plastic trays. Some wheatgrass growers prefer to plant in clear containers so they can see the impressive roots system develop.

Although drainage is important, you can use just about any flat vessel you like to plant wheatgrass. If the conditions are right it grows so quickly that many of the afflictions caused by poor drainage don't have the opportunity to take hold.

Whatever you choose, adequate drainage ensures the best growth, but this is one time that I'm not going to drone on about how it's mandatory. I've seen plenty of examples of gardeners who use old cake pans or Pyrex dishes (again, to show off the root system) for their wheatgrass and they do just fine. That's because wheatgrass, once it's established, is pretty hearty and grows quickly, which means there's less risk that you'll be watering it for months and risking root rot.

Prep Work

Wheatgrass tends to do best when it's soaked prior to planting, after first giving the seeds an initial rinse.

If you want to get deeper into eating sprouted greens (like alfalfa, broccoli, bean sprouts, etc.) then it might make sense to purchase a sprouting device, usually called a sprouter. There are some automatic sprouters available, but the most affordable options are often the manual devices that you can get for under $20. Some feature multiple trays for drainage, and you can even grow microgreens in them without a growing medium. A very simple option is the Easy Sprout, which looks like a plastic drinking cup and features a small seed insert and a base that catches excess rinse water.

Since I prefer to grow wheatgrass in vermiculite with a little compost mixed in, I just let my seeds soak in a bowl rather than utilizing a sprouter. There are several steps to the process:

- When preparing the seeds for soaking, add around three times as much water as you have seeds, since the seeds will absorb some of the water; filtered water tends to work best.
- Cover the bowl with a dishtowel or plastic wrap and let it soak for about eight hours or overnight.
- Drain the water, rinse the seeds until the water runs clear, and re-fill the bowl with another round of filtered water, letting it soak again for eight hours or overnight.
- Drain once more, rinse once more, and you guessed it: one more round of soaking, because for some reason, the third time is the charm.
- After that third night of soaking, drain the water and give it one more rinse; the seeds should have fine, wispy, hair-like roots jutting out from the seed.

For soil mix prep, it's sometimes useful to premoisten the soil, especially if your house tends to be dry.

When blending water and soil mix, go for a consistency that's like a crumbly brownie mix—then pick up a handful and squeeze. If a few drops of water come out, that's perfect. If there's a steady stream of water, it means you've made the mixture too wet, and you should add more dry mix. You'll only

Soaking wheatgrass seeds helps them to germinate quickly.

need a thin layer of this mix for the wheatgrass, and you can add vermiculite to encourage drainage.

Planting and Care

First Steps

If you're using a tray or pot with drainage holes, put a paper towel in the bottom first before adding soil. This ensures that the roots won't extend through the holes and attempt to take hold of whatever surface is below the tray. This seems to happen whenever I've forgotten the paper towels, and since I sometimes set my plants on a metal grid, like an old cooling rack used for baking, I always end up having to pry wheatgrass roots out of the rack.

On top of the paper towel, spread about 2 inches of your soil mix, making sure that's even but not pressed down firmly, which causes compaction.

Spread the seeds evenly across the top of the soil mix, and sow them heavily. Like microgreens and shoots, the seeds can be thickly sown to make harvest easier and growing more efficient. Press the seeds gently into the soil, but don't press them down to the point that they go beneath the soil's surface. Water the tray lightly—I usually do a heavy mist to make sure I'm not introducing too much water.

To protect the seedlings, cover the tray with another tray, a plastic dome lid, or some wet newspaper with small holes poked in it to allow for airflow.

If you are growing in a tray with drainage holes, line the tray with paper toweling first to keep the roots from growing out of the container.

Wheatgrass responds well to the wet newspaper strategy, which I only utilize for growing that little crop, because I find it too messy otherwise.

For the first few days, make sure to mist at least twice per day, keeping the soil moist but not soaked. Also give the newspaper a good spritz so that it doesn't dry out. If the growth is pushing up against the newspaper sheet, then switch to a taller cover, like an inverted tray or dome lid.

About three to five days after planting you should see significant sprouting, to the point that it pushes up the inverted tray, and the grass is about 2 inches tall. It may be yellowish at this stage, but don't worry, it will green up quickly with some light.

At this stage, move the tray to an area with indirect sunlight. Direct sun often "burns" the wheatgrass, so a shady spot is ideal.

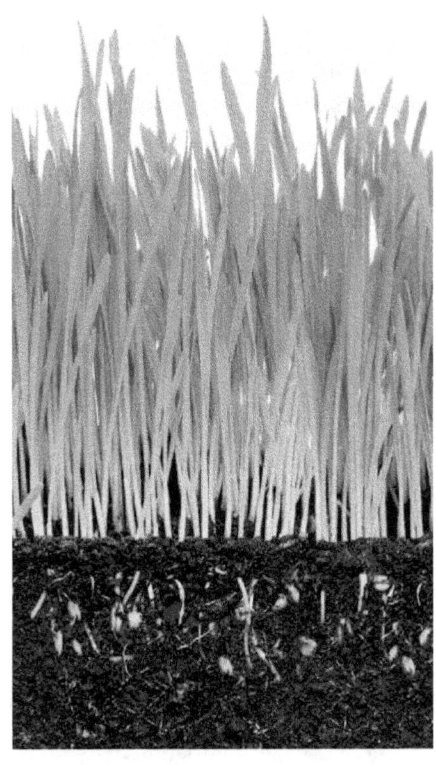

(ABOVE) The grass will grow steadily upright, and look like a very thick, very green shag carpet, and you can harvest in only about five to ten days after planting, depending on the stage you choose. (BELOW) If you've triple-rinsed the wheatgrass seeds and prepared the growing medium properly you should have sprouts within three to five days.

Maintaining Growth

One of the best aspects of wheatgrass is that it's a very low maintenance plant. You can spray some kelp fertilizer on the greens or in the soil if it seems like it could use a boost, but otherwise, just make sure to keep the soil mix moist with a heavy mist once per day.

Here are some other tips on getting the most out of your growing adventure:

- Always have several trays going in different stages of growth. In order to juice wheatgrass, you need a lot of shoots. Some people use an entire tray for just one juicing session, and it doesn't make very much, compared to vegetables like carrots or beets. For that reason, it's a good idea to time your harvest and growing cycles to get in the rhythm of having another tray growing while you harvest from your first one, and also a bowl of seeds soaking so you can plant more before that second tray reaches maturity.

- If you plan on storing your wheatgrass in the fridge rather than juicing or blending it immediately (see "Storage Considerations" on page 81 for more info), refrain from misting or watering for at least twelve hours before harvest. If the grass seems dry, you can water the soil, just make sure that the grass itself isn't moist, because even a small amount of moisture can affect storage times and make your harvest a quickly deteriorating mess in the fridge.

- Keep airflow steady, especially during humid months. The biggest challenge that crops up with wheatgrass is mold, and this can happen when the air is humid, the tray is overwatered, and there's no air circulation in the room. Putting fans in strategic locations can help enormously. The easiest way to tell if you already have a mold issue is to check the base of the grass blades—mold will appear as white tufts. If this is happening, remove all diseased grasses and refrain from eating the wheatgrass until you've determined that mold isn't present in the rest of the tray. Since you won't be cooking the wheatgrass, it's especially important to make sure that mold isn't present in anything you're consuming.

Troubleshooting

Some common problems and potential solutions for wheatgrass:

Only Some of the Seeds Are Sprouting

During the initial soaking and sprouting process, it's important to give the seeds some room to sprout. They don't require a vast amount, but they should get some space. Usually when only some of the seeds are sprouting, it's because I've tried using too much seed for one bowl, so they end up too dense and it stunts their germination. Another issue may be age of the seeds. Like so many things, seeds are cheaper when bought in bulk, and considering the amount of wheatgrass seed needed to create a lush bed, buying in larger quantities often makes sense. But when projects get put on hold and seeds age, sometimes germination can be affected.

Sprouted Seeds Don't Seem to Establish in the Tray during the Initial Growth Period

This often happens when I get lazy about rinsing the seeds during the soaking process. It's a crucial step, because otherwise your seeds are subject to rot. Essentially, if you don't rinse until the water runs clear, and you don't change the water consistently, you're starting to ferment your seeds, and that will severely stunt growth if you manage to get any growth at all.

Growth Seems Sluggish

The nice thing about wheatgrass is that it's meant to be speedy in terms of growth, so if you're waiting and waiting for the magic to happen, it usually means something has gone awry. Check the soil to make sure that it's well watered but not soaked, and that the tray is positioned in indirect light. If those factors are in place, then it might be because you've seeded too heavily, the room is too cold, or you lack air circulation. Try using a heat mat under the tray if room temperature is the culprit, and place a fan so that it's blowing near—but not directly on—the wheatgrass. If growth is still impacted, then it's probably heavy seeding, and you can keep this in mind when doing your next round.

Grasses Are Staying Yellow Even Though I've Removed the Cover

There's indirect light and then there's deep shade—when the grasses stay yellow, it's likely that you have the tray too far from a light source, so they can't take advantage of the photosynthesis process to "green up." They would still be edible, but weakened and not as nutrient-dense. Simply move the tray to a location where there's more indirect light, such as to the side of a window, or near a fluorescent light but not under it.

Tips Are Getting Brown and Dry

The opposite problem of yellowing is browning, and it's also related to light. In this case, it's likely that the tray is receiving too much direct light either by being put under a fluorescent or in a window space that receives direct sunlight. Essentially, you're cooking the plant in either case. I've found that this often happens when people place the tray in indirect sunlight in the morning, and then leave for work—because they're not home in the middle of the day, they don't know the light pattern shifts for that particular area, and by the time they get back, the plant is once again in indirect light. But it's possible that it could be getting full sun for a few hours per day, which will start the browning process. Some direct sun is fine, and can actually help green up some trays, but too much is a detriment.

Mold and More Mold

Although we've covered this briefly in the previous section, it's worth putting more strategies in place to prevent and deal with mold, since it can be hellaciously prevalent in some growing systems. Here are some more tips on dealing with the issue:

- Soak your seeds for a shorter amount of time; if your house is humid, you may want to soak for only about six hours.
- If the problem seems chronic through multiple rounds of growing, try adding grapefruit seed extract or citrus seed extract to your soak water—about 10 drops should suffice.
- Move the growing trays to a cooler location, like a basement; be sure to put lights and fans in place for the new grow space.
- Consider waiting for cooler weather to continue growing; if all else fails, aim for spring or fall for planting to avoid humidity issues. You can always grow a massive amount of wheatgrass during these times and then freeze the juice (see Storage Considerations section) for consumption during the summer.

Harvesting and Preservation

Getting Ready to Pick

You can harvest the grass at any point in its lifecycle, and you may want to experiment with taste, to see if you prefer younger wheatgrass when it's only about 3 or 4 inches tall, or if you like the mature stage at around 6 inches tall.

Once they reach the mature stage, the grassy shoots will "split," which means that a second blade of grass starts growing out of the initial blade of grass. This is the most common time for harvesting, because when it gets longer than this, the taste becomes woody and you risk yellowing of the stems, which is an indication of nutrient loss.

To harvest, grasp a small section by the top and then clip the grass just above the root level. You can harvest only as much as you need, and spread out the harvest time over a few days if desired.

Just be sure to keep watering the wheatgrass that's remaining, as well as the areas where you've harvested. Often, you can get a "second crop" that sprouts from seeds late in germinating. In some cases, you might see a third rotation of growth, but taste these sprouts before using them—they can sometimes have significantly more grassy flavor than the first harvest round. If you're throwing them in a green smoothie or juicing with other

Wheatgrass or pet grass is ready to harvest when the plants are 3" or 4" high—just cut the grass near the roots with scissors.

fruits and vegetables, this may not be important to you, but if you're hooked on wheatgrass shots, it could be a major difference from the taste you prefer.

Storage Considerations

Wheatgrass itself isn't usually an ingredient in dishes, and is used instead in juicing or in making smoothies. Because of that, the best way to prepare it is to cut it fresh, throw it in your blender or juicer (you may need a special attachment for the grass, depending on model) and drink it immediately.

When you cut it and then try to store it, there tends to be a loss in nutrient density, which is why you're growing it in the first place, so just make it easy on yourself and only have it fresh. That said, maybe a whole tray is mature and you want to catch it before it gets too grassy—in that case, dry out grasses by refraining from misting for twelve

Cut wheatgrass can simply be pureed in a blender to create juice, or you can use a hand-operated or power juicer. Whichever way you choose, be sure to juice the grass as soon as possible after picking it.

hours, harvest, then put in a glass container or plastic bag and keep in the crisper drawer of your fridge.

Another good tactic is to use a produce storage bag, which I utilize often when I know that I need to keep vegetables fresh for longer periods of time. These bags, found at co-ops and other stores, look like tiny laundry bags, with a thin mesh and a drawstring. Because they allow the vegetables, shoots, and sprouts to "breathe" while in the fridge, they prolong freshness.

You can also employ a very easy storage method by blending or juicing wheatgrass by itself, then putting the juice into ice cube trays. When they're frozen, pop them out and put them into a plastic freezer bag. These are great when blending up green smoothies, because they give you the fresh wheatgrass nutrition and flavor, and thicken up the smoothie, too.

SPROUTS

When you're short on space and resources, sprouts make an easy indoor growing project. Basically, you just need seeds, a glass jar (more on that soon), some cheesecloth or a thin dishtowel and voila! You're on your way to becoming a sprout expert.

Nutritionally, sprouts are also packed with enzymes, fiber, amino acids, vitamins, and other goodies that help boost your immune system and keep your health on track. Plus, they're delicious and quite simple to grow on a continual basis.

I tend to take on a sprout growing session in the depths of winter, when other plants might be slowing in their progress. In a Minnesota February, even microgreens will take longer to turn from seed into lush green carpet, so sprouts help me to get a nutritional charge while I'm waiting. Not all sprouts appeal to me in terms of taste, though, and it's likely that you'll make the same discovery—for me, I like sprouts with a kick like mustard or radish, but those with a more earthy taste (like alfalfa) just aren't my groove. And that's okay, because there are plenty of options when it comes to choosing what type of sprouts to grow, and finding out what you like is part of the sprouting adventure.

Sprouted soy beans are one of the most popular (and easy to grow) types of sprouts. They are good for garnishes but also good by the bowlful.

Good Varieties for Indoor Growing

There are many choices when it comes to sprouting, and much like microgreens, they encompass a sizeable chunk of the vegetable kingdom. You can sprout dill seeds, fenugreek, chives, peas, wheat, and tons of others. As you get more confident in your sprout setup, you can play around with different options, but in terms of getting started, these are some popular choices:

- *Alfalfa:* This one is the classic sprout, with a mild and nutty flavor, and it makes a nice starting point for sprouting.

Before and after: Alfalfa seeds and sprouts

- *Broccoli:* Research from Johns Hopkins University noted that broccoli sprouts present an "exceptionally rich source of inducers of enzymes that protect against chemical carcinogens." Plus: tasty.

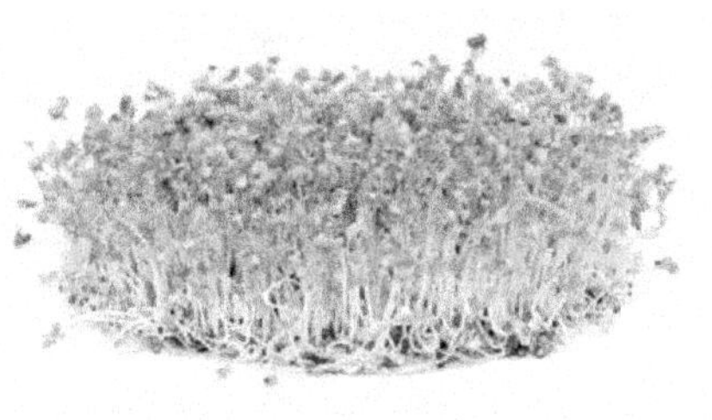

Sprouted broccoli seeds

- *Mung bean:* Many types of beans can be sprouted, and this is one of the most sprouted. Personally, I'm not a fan of the taste, but I've talked to people who eat them every day and find them rich and flavorful.

Before and after: Mung beans and sprouts

- *Blends:* If you look online for sprouts at locations like Sprout-people.com, you'll find a number of mixes with multiple types of seeds, and this is always a nice option. For example, an "Italian Blend" will pair clover, garlic, and cress, or a grain mix might include wheat, rye, oats, kamut, and quinoa. These are usually a very cost-effective way to get multiple types of seeds without buying them individually.

Clover and radish sprouts

- *Others:* In theory, you can sprout any seed you wish. In practice, of course, some just taste better than others. In addition to the other sprouts on this page sprout seed catalogs and retailers sell some of the following: fenugreek, daikon radish, edamame beans, kale, sunflower, buckwheat, and onions.

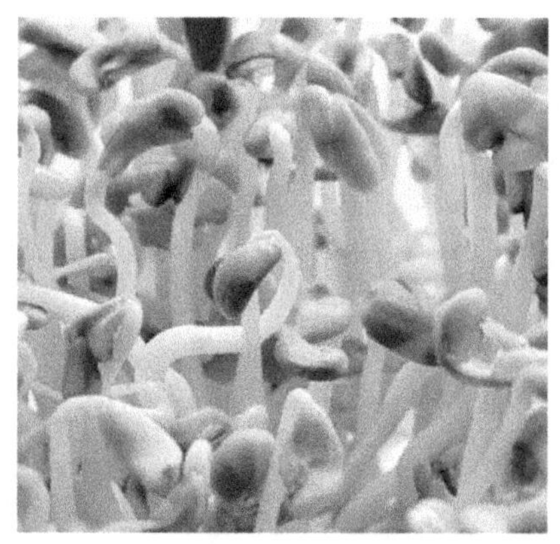
Fenugreek

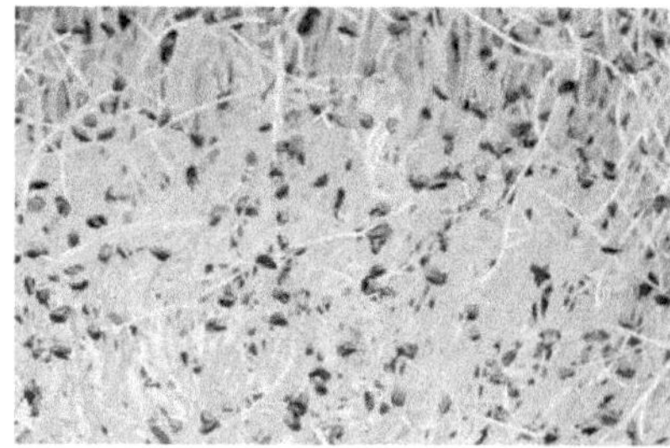
Onion

Daikon radish

'Red Russian' kale

Trays, Pots, and Other Containers

There are plenty of options when it comes to abundant sprout growth, and check out the Resources page in the back of the book for some good sites to peruse for supplies.

If you plan on growing sprouts often, consider getting a sprouter. These devices range from a small, cup-like container that's usually around $10 to a multitray sprouter that lets you grow numerous types of sprouts simultaneously.

These larger sprouters can be fun, creating little sprout skyscrapers in your kitchen, but keep in mind that you'll need to really stay on top of the process if you have multiple sprout types growing on different timeframes. Sprouts aren't difficult to grow, but they do require specific care done at regular intervals, so unlike shoots or even microgreens, you can't start them and then go away for a few days. But if you're turning into a sprout enthusiast and your counter is taken up by too many jars and containers, a multitray sprouter may be just what you need.

However, if you're just getting started and you want to experiment with just one sprout variety at a time, then simplify your setup by utilizing only a glass jar (I use a quart-sized Mason or Ball jar) and some cheesecloth or a thin dishtowel for placing over

For small-scale sprouting, and a kickstart to your sprouting efforts, a sprouter can be helpful. There are many types of sprouters for sale today. The one above is European and features three small round sprouting trays.

An assortment of seeds sold and packaged specifically for sprouting.

the top. The sprouting seeds will need some air circulation but will be sensitive to dust, so refrain from using a heavier lid, since it will trap moisture.

(ABOVE) A more common sprouter is simply a glass jar with a metal mesh lid that aids in straining. (BELOW) Any small jar can be used for making sprouts just as effectively as special sprouters. Cleaning and rinsing can be more time consuming than when using a sprouter, however.

Prep Work

First, make sure your jar or sprouter is clean. And I mean *clean*. Sprouts are already susceptible to mold issues, so don't take a chance by thinking that a few dried flecks of food or some dust won't be a big deal. You don't need to bleach the container, but take a few moments to examine it thoroughly after washing and make sure that it's ready. When prepping containers for sprouting, I prefer hand-washing them to using my dishwasher because I feel that they get a better scrub that way.

Planting and Care

First Steps

Put about a tablespoon of seeds in your jar or container and cover them with several inches of warm water. I tend to use filtered water since I find I get better results that way, but sometimes use tap water if I'm in a rush. Here are steps from there:

- Let the seeds soak overnight, or up to twenty-four hours if you're sprouting larger seeds like beans.
- In the morning, or after the soak period, drain all of the water, preferably though the cheesecloth so it acts as a filter.
- Fill the jar with a few more inches of fresh water, and immediately drain again through the filter.
- Place in an area with indirect light.
- Put in fresh water again, and this time place the jar back on your counter.

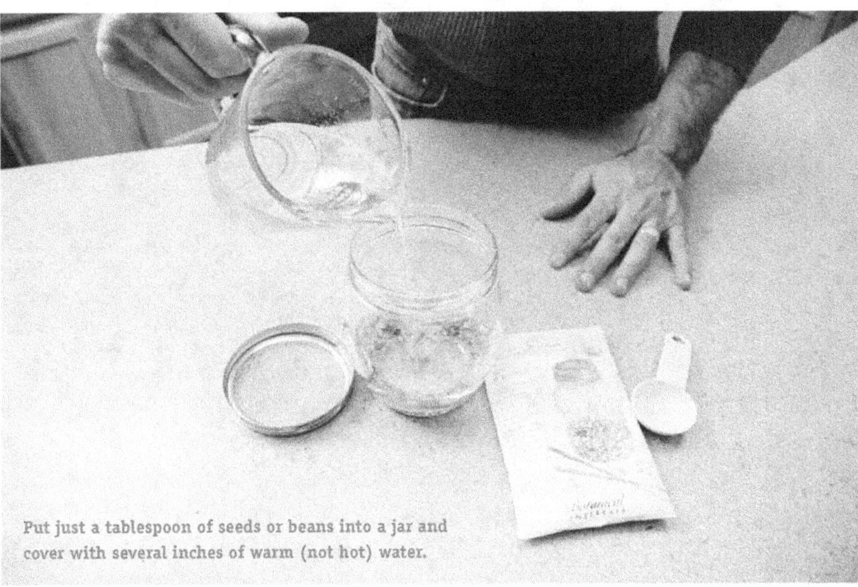

Put just a tablespoon of seeds or beans into a jar and cover with several inches of warm (not hot) water.

- Repeat this process—drain, refill to rinse, drain again, fill with fresh water—every morning and evening (every twelve hours, roughly) for the next four to six days, until the sprouts have grown to a stage where you're ready to harvest them.

- Before eating, give the sprouts one last rinse, and get as much water out of them as you can. Then you can simply place the jar in the refrigerator.

(ABOVE LEFT) Drain the seeds by pouring water out through the mesh sprouter lid. Or, a cheesecloth cover on a glass jar helps airflow, and also makes a handy strainer when draining and rinsing your seeds. (ABOVE RIGHT) Always keep sprouts in indirect light when first growing them, so they don't "burn" in the sunlight.

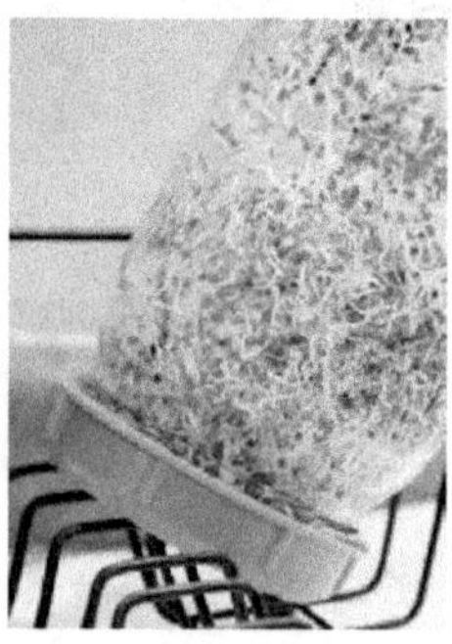

(FAR LEFT) Rinsing sprouting seeds is a vital part of the process—otherwise, you can introduce bacteria that will wipe out your efforts. (LEFT) Give sprouts a final rinse and let them drain before you eat them up.

Troubleshooting

Some common problems and potential solutions for sprouts:

Mold Forms in the Jar

Of all the problems with sprouts, this is the largest. You really have to stay on top of the rinsing schedule, because otherwise, you'll end up with a mushy, moldy mess and will have to start over. If that happens, throw out the sprouts (even if they have a very small mold patch) and start again, being sure to sterilize the jar before you do. If the problem keeps happening, consider using a different container for your sprouting, such as a sprouter or a tray.

Sprouts Seem to Be Taking Longer than Four to Six Days

If you're living in a colder climate, sprouts can take a little longer to reach maturity. You can speed up the process by first soaking the seeds overnight before placing them in a sprouter or jar. This will help the seeds to germinate faster. Also, you can choose a sprout type that will be on a faster schedule, like beans. This category includes kidney beans, adzuki beans, cowpeas, garbanzos, and lentils. Beans often take only about two to four days from sprout to maturity.

Sprouts Are Growing, but Don't Seem to Be "Greening Up"

Although sprouts are fine in an area with indirect light, sometimes they need a boost of photosynthesis. If your sprouts are not getting green, move the container to a location with better light, or near a window. Just make sure it's not in direct sunlight, since that can dry out the sprouts. Also, keep in mind that not all sprouts will be green. For example, mung beans are a pretty, translucent white when fully sprouted, with a yellowed tip that results from the seed husk.

Harvesting and Preservation

Getting Ready to Pick

When you "harvest" sprouts, it just means you pull them out of the glass container and eat them. What could be easier? Just make sure that they pass the smell test— even if I've eaten from a jar of sprouts at breakfast, I'll smell them before putting them on my salad at dinner.

That's because there are often warnings about sprouts being associated with outbreaks of *Salmonella* and *E. coli,* which can happen if the sprouts are allowed to sit in water for too long. When that occurs, bacteria can form and the tender sprouts are vulnerable.

You can store your sprouts in the same jar you sprouted them in as long as you refrigerate them. But don't wait more than a day or two to eat them.

I've found that smelling the sprouts before eating prevents issues. If they are off in any way, the aroma is detectable, in my experience. When in doubt, *always* throw it out.

Storage Considerations

Sprouts don't store well, and even when you put the jar in the refrigerator, the longest shelf life you're going to get is about a week. Even then, that might be pushing it. The sprouts will begin to show deterioration by getting a little mushy, and before long mold will form. The best tactic with sprouts is to eat them within a day or two after they're fully grown.

MUSHROOMS

A Little Forest Right on Your Countertop

For me, mushrooms always have a little bit of mystery to them. Maybe it's because I grew up eating only the slimy, canned mushrooms that came already sliced, thrown into a casserole. The only other mushroom encounters I had as a kid were the occasional fleck in a can of cream of mushroom soup—and believe me, if you live in the Midwest, you're likely to consume your weight in cream of mushroom soup, since it forms the base of about 75 percent of potluck dishes (the rest is Jell-O).

So, when I finally ate "real" mushrooms as an adult, it was a revelation. These days, I seek out exotic mushrooms and befriend people who forage for them. Also, when you're standing at the co-op and looking at the astronomical price of morels, you probably say, "Who would pay that much for mushrooms?" The answer is: me.

It seems logical that I'd be keen to grow them indoors, and I've made many attempts to keep a wide range of mushrooms, but to be honest, there are only a few varieties that really work well (see the varieties section for more info) in my space. I've tried to keep logs inoculated with shiitake spawn in my basement, but it can be very tricky to keep humidity and airflow levels perfect if you're trying to grow from logs indoors. Let's take a few easier routes instead.

Good Media for Indoor Growing

When choosing which type of mushroom you want to grow, it's important to select spawn (which is what mushroom "starter" is called) that works well with whatever medium you've chosen. For example, oyster mushrooms grow best in straw, while wine caps do well in sawdust. So when making a choice, pick your medium first, and then find out what mushrooms grow well in it. Here's a quick cheat sheet:

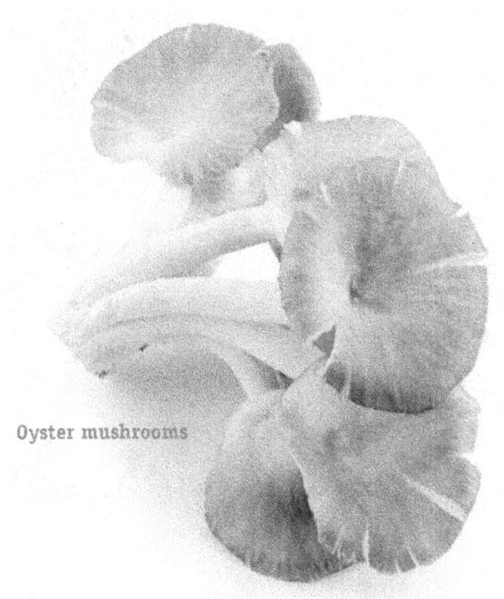

Oyster mushrooms

- *Sawdust:* The benefit of using sawdust is that it's economical and you can usually purchase small bags of it at a garden store. Be sure to get the fine-grained sawdust as opposed to the material that's closer to woodchips. The mushrooms that do well in this medium are shiitake and wine cap.

- *Straw:* Because it holds moisture well but also allows for a nice amount of airflow, straw is a nice medium for mushrooms, and oyster mushrooms grow particularly well in straw. There are several types of straw, but wheat straw tends to be the best for growing.

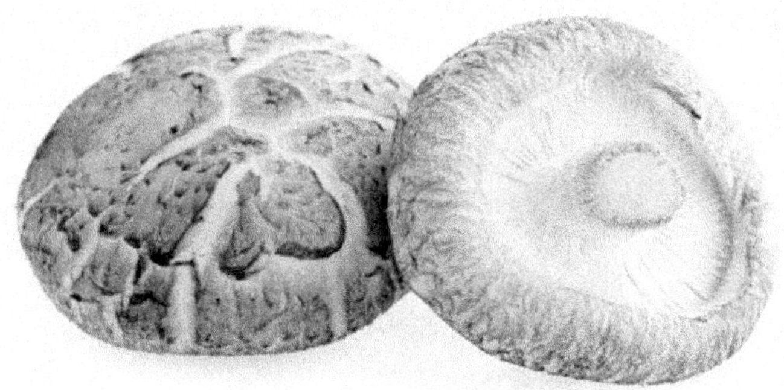

Shiitake mushroom

Inoculated log with shiitake mushrooms

- *Hardwood block:* One great option for first-time growers is a "table top farm," which comes as a portion of an inoculated log, or contained in a hardwood sawdust block. You simply need to water, adjust humidity levels as instructed, and enjoy. These blocks have limited fruiting times, unlike some of the spawn grown in straw or sawdust, but they also tend to have better success rates. You purchase preinoculated logs for around $30-$40: these will yield a dozen or so shiitakes every three weeks once the fruiting begins. Or, you can inoculate your own log or logs with shiitake spawn.

One thing to keep in mind when ordering is that many mushroom spawn providers will only ship during certain

Other systems for growing mushrooms include kits such as this. To grow oyster mushrooms with this, you simply cut open the book, add moisture, and the mushrooms will appear in a week or two.

times of the year. For example, major supplier Field & Forest will ship mushroom kits only from November until May, although it does ship certain types of spawn year round.

Also, be sure to buy spawn instead of spores. It's possible to use spores (which are like seeds) for indoor growing, as opposed to spawn, which is more like buying transplants with roots already formed, but it takes quite a bit of experience, patience, and time to grow from spores.

Prep Work

If you're using straw as a mushroom medium, here's where it's going to get a little weird. To reduce the chance of disease issues, it's best to pasteurize the straw, and for that, you need to cook it. I'm not kidding.

Put a large pot of water on the stove, and let it boil for around twenty minutes while you're chopping the straw down to a more manageable size, generally about 1 to 3 inches. I usually just grab a handful of straw, hold it over a bowl, and then cut it with a scissors so I get 2-inch strands. Some people use a blender or food processor, but I've found the cleanup from that procedure to be too time consuming.

When the water's been boiling for a while, lower the temperature to just under a boil, and use a meat thermometer to check the water temp, which should be between 160 and 170 degrees Fahrenheit. Then, add the straw to the water, and force any floating straw (there will be plenty) under the water with a slotted spoon. Ideally, all the straw should remain under the water, so if you can, weight the straw with a small grate, Pyrex dish, or other heat-resistant item.

Keep checking the temperature of the water to make sure it stays within range, and "cook" the straw for about 45 minutes. Then, turn off the stove, let the straw cool down for about 10 minutes, and then drain the water from the pot.

1. Chop straw into small strips to make handling easier.

Don't throw away the water—you can use it as "straw juice" for your mushrooms later, giving them a nutritional kick. Remove the straw from the pot, and let it come to room temperature before spawning. It will begin to dry, but it's helpful to have the straw still be somewhat wet when introducing the spawn.

You can also buy pasteurized straw, but where's the fun in that? This way, your kitchen can smell "farmy" for at least a day or two.

2. Put chopped-up straw into the boiling water.

3. Drain water from the pot of straw, and be sure to keep the straw water so you can use it later—it can add a nutritional boost to your mushrooms.

Planting and Care

First Steps

Wash your hands and prep area thoroughly. Mushroom spawn is susceptible to disease, and having a clean environment is particularly important.

Shred your straw or evenly spread your sawdust in your container, and then mix in some used coffee grounds. If you're a tea drinker, it's worth it to pop into a nearby coffee shop and ask for a small bucket of grounds—they usually throw them away anyway, and many shops near urban gardening efforts are used to those type of requests.

The coffee grounds are packed with nutrients that provide a major boost to your mushroom spawn, and they also help to reduce the number of microorganisms that could compete with your spawn.

Your spawn will usually look like a block of very old cheese. Break this up into very small crumbles and integrate with the straw or sawdust. In some cases, the spawn will already be

4. Coffee grounds are a great way to get more nutrition to your mushrooms, without much expense.

5. Crumble the spawn if it arrives in a block.

in sawdust, so you just have to add it to another, thicker layer of the stuff.

In terms of a container, you can use a variety of containers, but one of the most popular methods is to pack a plastic bag with the medium and spawn, and then poke holes into it every three inches or so. This will allow airflow, while still keeping the whole bundle warm and moistened.

Alternately, you can use a tray or baking pan and spread the mixture evenly, which gives the mushrooms more room to grow. Sprinkle some potting soil over the top, and then mist thoroughly. Place the pan or bag in a cool, dark spot, such as a basement. You can also use a garage as long as the temperature is around 50 degrees Fahrenheit.

Mist the mixture periodically if it looks like it's starting to get dry. You may begin to see a whitish fuzz develop—don't worry, it's not mold. For mushrooms, mold is most likely to be black, pink, yellow, or bluish green.

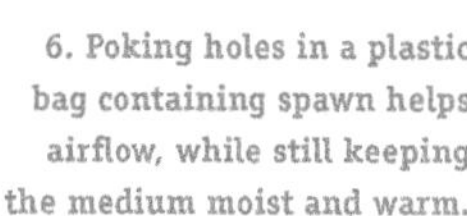
6. Poking holes in a plastic bag containing spawn helps airflow, while still keeping the medium moist and warm.

Option: Instead of a bag you can add your straw mixture to a pan or plate and top it off with a layer of potting soil after the spawn has been introduced.

Troubleshooting

Some common problems and potential solutions for mushrooms:

No Initial Growth Occurring

This can happen when an area is too cool or you don't have enough moisture. If you've been misting the mushrooms on a regular basis, try putting a germination mat under your container. If the problem is moisture, try placing a damp towel over the container for a few days so that moisture can be contained more efficiently. Don't leave it on for too long, though, since the mushrooms need some fresh air to prevent carbon dioxide buildup.

Multiple Mushroom Growing Attempts, Without Any Results

Maybe you've tried both straw and sawdust, you've changed your containers, tried different rooms in the house and corners of the basement, maybe even sung to the spawn. And still, you're getting nothing. Unfortunately, this can happen even with temperature and moisture control. In this case, you may want to invest in an indoor mushroom kit. I promise, this isn't cheating. These kits are very well designed for growing, and often put together by mycologists (mushroom experts) who are super savvy about creating options for indoor environments. Choose a kit that's either one of the "table top farm" varieties, or just a simple bag filled with spawn and sawdust (sometimes with coffee thrown in) that only needs to be watered at regular intervals.

Harvesting and Preservation

Getting Ready to Harvest

Depending on the variety, mushrooms should be ready for some harvesting at about three weeks. Usually, the best sign of maturity is that the caps will separate from the stems. At that stage, just pick them by hand.

Shiitake mushrooms grow in clusters once the inoculated mushroom log is activated.

Store your harvested mushrooms in a paper bag and refrigerate them.

Storage Considerations

Don't wash the mushrooms until you're ready to prepare them for a meal—this will allow them to last longer. Place them in a brown paper bag (never in a plastic one), and store in the refrigerator. A plastic container will trap moisture, whereas the paper bag absorbs any excess moisture coming off the mushrooms. If you need to store mushrooms for longer, consider dehydrating them or cook them and then freeze them.

Radishes, Carrots, Tomatoes, and Other Crops

Radishes, Carrots, Tomatoes, and Other Crops

Many plants with a shallow root system can grow well indoors, such as beets, radishes, some varieties of carrots, lettuces, and with the right conditions, even hot peppers and tomatoes.

With these types of crops, it's even more important to establish good growing practices as outlined in Part One of this book—proper airflow, a robust indoor soil mix, good lighting, pest prevention, and appropriate containers.

With a designated growing area set up correctly, the fun can begin. Although growing mini-crops like pea shoots is a jaunty endeavor, I find deep satisfaction in nurturing indoor vegetables that take time to develop, rewarding me with a plate filled with lush salad greens, sweet carrots, peppery radishes, and other bounty from my kitchen garden.

Especially in the spring, when I'm craving fresh greens but only find West Coast (or internationally shipped) options in my grocery store, I feel inspired to go on a planting frenzy, filling up every available space with shelves, lights, and just-seeded pots.

Not every vegetable is perfect for my kitchen counter, though. I've tried many varieties that might start out fine but lack the soil depth needed, or that thrive better outdoors in the field.

Here, we'll cover the different varieties of crops that make the most sense for indoor growing, and take a look at special considerations in terms of soil, pest prevention, containers, and lighting. Much like the preparation for faster-growing plants like microgreens and pea shoots, successful growing and harvesting of indoor crops is all about good upfront work, paying attention, and maintaining that all-important sense of adventure.

(OPPOSITE PAGE) Potted vegetables with relatively shallow roots can succeed in an in-home growing setting. Here, a pot of cilantro and a tray of pea shoots are nestled in among larger veggies, including Swiss chard, kale, and spinach.

LETTUCES

Even before I started farming, I was a salad kind of girl. That label evolved over time, though: growing up, "salad" was a wedge of iceberg lettuce with ranch dressing and little else (we'll sidestep the fact that in Minnesota, "salad" can also be Jell-O and Cool Whip), but eventually I made my way to a huge variety of greens, including red oakleaf, butterhead, bibb, and romaine.

I love the blend of textures and colors you can put together with salad mixes, especially with choices like the 'Freckles' variety that grows with deep splashes of crimson or 'Rhazes,' which forms tight heads of red leaves that hide a solid lime green center.

A lettuce bowl isn't just a way of serving greens at the table: it is also a way of growing replenishable lettuces indoors.

There are so many options when it comes to lettuce variety that it only seems right to kick off the crops chapter with this versatile and much-loved vegetable.

(CLOCKWISE FROM TOP RIGHT) A variety of small, potted lettuces; rows of red and green leaf lettuce; a variety of potted organic salad greens; green leaf lettuce; 'Lollo Bionda' lettuce.

Get Ready

Good Varieties for Indoor Growing

At the risk of oversimplifying the range of lettuce choices, I'll make a general claim: lettuce tends to come in one of two versions—either you have head lettuce that's true to that definition, or you have salad mixes that combine a number of varieties and grow in a cluster rather than a tightly contained head.

That doesn't mean that they're two distinct types—head lettuces can be included in a mix, you just harvest them when they're still petite greens. The difference comes during the seeding process, because you either space them to accommodate for head lettuce growth in those varieties, or you seed liberally (though not as heavily as microgreens) so that you can harvest several varieties simultaneously.

When it comes to indoor growing, I nearly always gravitate to the mixes because they grow quickly, I can seed them according to pot size, and they incorporate a range of flavors from mustard greens and peppery arugula to pretty 'Rouge d'Hiver' and frilly 'Lollo Rosso.'

Many seed companies sell their own mixes (see Resources page at the end of the book), but you can also create your own from contenders like these:

- *Arugula:* Also known as rocket, this is a dependable choice for adding a peppery flavor to salads. The spiky, dark green leaves mix well in a salad but also can be substituted for spinach in some dishes.

Arugula

- *'Green Oakleaf' and 'Red Oakleaf':* Not surprisingly, these lettuces get their name for having leaves that are similar to those of oak trees. In this case, *oakleaf* is an umbrella term with several varieties in that family, such as 'Tango,' 'Bolsachica,' 'Panisse,' and my favorite, 'Sulu' (which I love because I'm a sci-fi nerd). Oakleaf varieties are very easy to grow, and tend to have a mild flavor and crunch.

'Red Oakleaf' lettuce

- *Baby leaf:* Much like oakleaf, "baby leaf" is a general term rather than a variety in itself. Designed to be harvested at an early stage of growth, some nice picks for baby leaf lettuce are 'Red Sails,' 'Refugio,' 'Parris Island,' and 'Defender.' Here's a head's up for seed ordering: some baby leaf options are also oakleaf varieties, but not all oakleaf choices are designated as baby leaf. Confused yet? Don't worry—the designation doesn't matter for growing, it's just a way to indicate which lettuces are best when harvested at a petite stage.

Baby leaf lettuce (Romaine)

- *'Lollo Rosso':* Incredibly frilly and slightly bitter, this lettuce has an intense flavor that gets stronger as it gets larger. The red leaves have a bright green splash near the bottom, and it tends to be best when mixed with milder lettuces rather than served solo.

'Lollo Rosso'

There are so very many varieties of lettuce that it's really a matter of taste and visual preference as to what you pick. I tend to like a bit of peppery flavor, a hint of bitterness, and an array of reds and greens. If you like only mild greens, opt for a single variety that promises that color and taste. If you can't decide and just want numerous seed varieties blended together, then go for one of the lettuce mixes offered by the seed companies that specialize in those.

No matter what you pick, I'd advise jotting down growing notes in a journal. When growing several varieties of lettuce, I sometimes forget what works well and what doesn't, or what tasted too bitter or too boring. A quick perusal of my gardening journal before ordering always helps me to distinguish the bountiful from the blah.

Trays, Pots, and Other containers

Because lettuce has a shallow root system, it works well in a medium-sized container. I tend to use hanging baskets because I can move them around more easily, and because they look nice as a focal point in the kitchen, especially if I'm growing lettuces with plenty of red leaves.

Like other plants, lettuce will do better in plastic than in terra cotta pots, because the clay will dry out the soil mix faster than the plastic. If you like the look of terra cotta, just pop a plastic insert into pot. Just make sure there are holes in the bottom for proper drainage.

Soil Mix

As long as you're not using soil from your garden, lettuces can thrive in a variety of soil types. You don't have to play around with drainage options by including rocks, or mixing sand into a compost blend—just grab a bag of all-purpose potting mix and you're good to go. Ideally, the mix should be organic and designated for vegetable growing.

(ABOVE) Sterile potting mix works just fine for potting indoor veggies. Organic products are available.

(BELOW) Plastic planters dry out less quickly than clay and tend to work out better for just about any plant, indoors or out. The oblong shape is perfect for a short row of lettuces.

Planting and Care

First Steps

Fill the pot with soil, with about an inch of space between the top of the container and the soil. Sprinkle the lettuce seeds on top of the soil, taking care to separate any that are too close to each other. For a medium-sized pot, you'll probably use about twenty seeds, but it's not necessary to be picky about it and count them out. You don't need to get anxious about spacing, either, as long as they aren't clumped together.

Sprinkle potting soil lightly over the top of the seeds, only enough to barely cover them. If the top cover of soil is too heavy, it will prevent light from boosting the germination.

Spray the seeds with water from a mister bottle so that soil is moist but not thoroughly soaked. Watering them directly from a watering can could cause the seeds to shift or to be driven farther down into the soil.

Continue to mist once per day, ideally in the morning. I make it into a habit by misting the lettuce seeds while I'm waiting for my first cup of coffee to brew; I know I'll never skip that java, so by tying the two activities together, it's easy to make sure I don't forget to hydrate the seeds. You should start to see germination in about one or two weeks, depending on varieties.

Maintaining Growth

Once the lettuces begin to establish, there are several tactics for fostering growth:

- Water every other day to keep the soil moist but not soaked. The way to tell if it needs water is to put your finger about half an inch into the soil and if it feels dry, then water.
- As lettuces get larger, it's usually better to bottom water. This means filling a sink or tray with a few inches of water and placing the lettuce pot into it for about ten minutes. Don't let the lettuce sit in water for a long time, or collect water in a plate under the pot; this can lead to root rot.
- You may notice that several lettuces are sprouting from the same area. Weed out the weaker seedlings so that the stronger ones can have more room to expand. If the weeded-out seedlings look viable at all, just transfer them to a separate pot or eat them as microgreens.
- Fertilize if growth seems slow. I don't usually use fertilizer for lettuces because they don't tend to need the boost, but if your lettuces are looking like they could use some extra nutrition, apply a fertilizer once a week for three weeks and see if that makes a difference. Don't apply more than that, though, or you could "burn" the plant through over-fertilization.

Troubleshooting

It's Been a Week and There's No Germination

If you've been watering faithfully and giving the lettuces enough sunlight, then be patient and wait another week; sometimes, in certain conditions, they can be sluggish in terms of germination but will establish fine once they start growing. If it's been a few weeks and there's no germination, you may be overwatering or setting the pot in a location that's too dark.

The Lettuces Seem Droopy

One of the nice things about living in the Midwest is that lettuces do well indoors because so much of the year is cool (maybe a little too much of the year for some folks). Lettuce loves cooler temperatures and will thrive most at around 60 to 70 degrees Fahrenheit. If you're experiencing higher humidity or temperatures in your house, try moving the lettuce to a cooler location.

Harvesting and Preservation

Getting Ready to Pick

Harvesting lettuces is a breeze—just snip them at whatever stage of growth appeals most to you. Usually, I prefer smaller lettuce greens rather than larger leaves, so I cut them when they're only about 6 inches high. No matter what size you choose, just be sure to avoid the inner leaves of each lettuce cluster, since it contains the immature growth that will lead to your next salad.

Storage Considerations

Like microgreens, lettuce tends to keep best in glass containers. They also do fine in plastic bags placed in the crisper drawer of the refrigerator. In general, though, it's better to harvest only what you need for a particular meal and let the plant keep generating lettuce leaves.

(BELOW) Whether it's a single plant or a whole row, lettuce grown indoors brightens the house and is a very convenient source of greens. (LOWER) Choose lettuce leaves on the outer part of the plant for picking. Let the inner ones stay so the plant continues to grow.

RADISHES

The best thing about growing radishes (indoors or out) is that they grow very quickly; sometimes they're ready to eat less than a month after planting.

Although I've always included lettuce in my food mix, radishes are a recent addition. In fact, despite significantly boosting my culinary expertise over the past decade (it's not hard to get better at cooking if you start out eating potato chips for dinner—from that base, anything is an improvement), I only began eating radishes when Karla and I grew them at Bossy Acres.

Radishes were our first crop to harvest, and I was shocked at how flavorful they were. I'd always believed that radishes were dry and peppery, based on the reactions of other people who said they hated the vegetable. But freshly harvested radishes—particularly those that aren't left in the field for too long—are actually somewhat juicy, and impart subtle flavors. Some have a kick, true, but those can be tamed with quick pickling (see storage notes later in this section).

For indoor gardeners, radishes can be a fun crop to grow, because they mature very quickly, sometimes in only about three weeks from seeding. You can eat the greens, and their bright colors (for most varieties) are a gorgeous addition to any kitchen garden.

Good Varieties for Indoor Growing

Because radishes are a root crop, you'll want to pick varieties that will fit in whatever container you choose. If you want to experiment with growing a long radish in a tall container, you could opt for a Daikon, which can grow up to 18 inches long and usually takes two months to mature. In general, though, I tend to like fast-growing varieties that don't take up much space. Here are some options for those:

Trays, Pots, and Other Containers

When choosing a container, you can plant several radishes in a round pot, but I tend to like a narrow, rectangular pot to mimic the way that radishes would grow in the field. They need to be at least a few inches apart for adequate growth, so putting them in a long container will create a nice row that's also visually appealing.

Prep Work

Consider planting radishes during a cooler part of the year, like late spring or early autumn. Although radishes planted indoors won't be as sensitive to sudden temperature changes the way they would outside, they do like cooler temps. That's why they're often one of the first crops to be harvested at the farm.

- *'French Breakfast':* More tapered rather than round, this is a popular variety for its white-tipped end and crunchy texture.

French Breakfast radishes

- *'Cherry Belle':* These mature in less than a month and tend to have a mild flavor. True to their name, they have a bright, cheery red exterior.

'Cherry Belle' radishes

In terms of soil, standard indoor potting mix will work, and just make sure that there's adequate drainage. This is one case where a little compost mixed into the soil would be beneficial, since radishes tend to like some added nutrients.

Planting and Care

First Steps

Sow the radish seeds about ½ inch deep, which usually means putting them in the soil and poking them down slightly. I like to place the seeds about 2 inches apart, with the recognition that I might need to "thin" them at some point to let the heartier radishes thrive.

Sprinkle some potting mix on top of the new seeds, and water so that the soil is dampened but not soaked. Place in a sunny spot, or under a full-spectrum fluorescent. To help with germination, create a "mini-greenhouse" environment by covering with plastic wrap for a few days until you begin to see them sprout. Once this starts, remove the wrap and mist with a spray bottle until the soil is moist.

(LEFT) Sow the radish seeds so they are ½ inch deep and about 2 inches apart. (BELOW RIGHT) After planting and topdressing with a light layer of potting mix, water the radishes and then stretch some plastic wrap over the pot for a couple of days.

Maintaining Growth

Here are some tips on getting your radishes from seed to harvest:

- Water regularly—unlike some crops that should be watered when the soil is particularly dry, radishes do well with a frequent, predictable watering schedule. This will help them to grow more quickly, which leads to a milder taste rather than the overly peppery, woody taste that occurs when radishes grow too slowly or are left for too long before harvest.
- Plant more in additional containers every few weeks—this is equivalent to crop rotation, but on a tiny scale. Planting on a continual basis will ensure that you always have radishes in progress to replace the ones you harvest, so you don't have to wait another month after picking to get more radishes.

Troubleshooting

Some common problems with radishes and potential solutions:

Leaves Are Brown and/or Drooping

Most likely, this is a light issue. Since radishes prefer cooler environments, try moving the pot to an area with more indirect sunlight, or moving it farther from its grow light.

Radishes Don't Seem to Have Enough Room to Grow

In the field, we plant radishes quite close together and then thin them later, so that the strongest are given the chance to thrive. This increases the yield on a harvest, but for a home garden effort, you don't need to plant them quite this intensively. If you do happen to experience crowding, simply pluck out the young radishes that seem weaker, and remember, you can eat the greens so that they don't go to waste.

My Radishes Are Tough and Taste Dry and Woody

There's not much that can be done at this point since they've already been harvested, but it's good to note for the future so that you can harvest them earlier next time. Some people believe radishes should be larger before they can be eaten, so they wait until the radishes are the size of small apples, but for most varieties, that's too large.

Pick radishes when they are still relatively small and tender.

Harvesting and Preservation

Getting Ready to Pick

Often, much like carrots, radishes will "shoulder" when they're ready to be picked. That means they push up out of the soil with part of the vegetable showing. This is hugely helpful in determining the size of the radish, which should be about an inch in diameter at harvest time.

If they aren't shouldering, gently dig into the soil with your finger until you can feel the top of the radish, and this will give you an idea of the size. If they're not ready, just replace whatever soil you've moved and check again in a few days.

Once they're ready for harvest, just take hold at the base of the leaves and give a firm tug. It doesn't take much effort, and they tend to pop out easily.

(ABOVE) Radishes are ready for picking when the shoulder is about an inch across—don't let them get any bigger, as they tend to get woody. (BELOW) For most of us, one or two sharp-flavored radishes go a long way, making them a great choice for indoor, small-space planting.

Storage Considerations

If you'll be storing radishes instead of eating them immediately, just brush the soil off and store them instead of washing them right away. This helps to keep them fresh for longer.

Radishes last for weeks if stored in a plastic bag in the crisper drawer, but my favorite tactic is to create a quick pickle that doesn't require any canning equipment; you simply store it in the refrigerator. This is the only recipe I'll include in the book, because during the farm season, it's what I make on a weekly basis, and I feel like it really brings out the flavor of the radishes.

Sweet Pickled Radishes

10 radishes (equaling about a pound)
½ cup apple cider vinegar
¼ cup honey
¼ cup raw sugar
¼ cup filtered water
2 Tbsp canning salt
2 Tbsp mustard seed
2 tsp ground ginger
1 tsp turmeric
1 garlic clove, thinly sliced

1. Scrub radishes and cut off their "tails" and root ends, no need to peel. Slice thinly or in chunks.
2. Combine remaining ingredients and bring to a boil; cook until sugar and honey have dissolved, then turn down to low simmer.
3. Put radish slices in glass canning jars (such as Mason or Ball) and pack tightly.
4. Pour hot liquid over radishes and use a spoon (poke it into the jar) to remove air bubbles.
5. Put in fridge, and let "set" for at least eight hours before eating.

Note: You can adjust spices based on what you have on hand, or reduce the sugar if you find it's too sweet or you want more radish flavor. Because these are "fridge pickles" they're not subject to the kind of rigor needed for standard canning projects.

CARROTS

To be honest, carrots grown in containers can be tricky, but you can boost your chance of success by choosing the right varieties. My favorites in the field tend to be rainbow carrots, with their long tapers of pinkish red or dark crimson, both cut open to reveal a rich orange inside.

As much as I'd love to plant those type of full, luscious beauties inside, however, it just doesn't make much sense to utilize that much soil and lug around a large container just for the thrill of growing larger carrots indoors. I get my fix instead from smaller varieties, and also from growing just one or two pots at a time.

Would I like to turn my office space into a carrot-filled zone, with radishes and hot peppers on the periphery? Of course I would. Maybe someday I'll decide never to sell my house and start building raised beds in less-used spaces.

With their intense flavor (compared to grocery store carrots), carrots grown in-home go a long way when seasoning soups.

I'll be that weird lady who gets raided by the DEA because a neighbor sees massive grow lights in every room.

Until that time, though, let's go with carrots that make sense for a small-scale growing plan.

Good Varieties for Indoor Growing

Resist the temptation to grow your own juicing garden (unless you actually do have an indoor greenhouse, and in that case, full speed ahead to you) and opt for varieties that are more round than tapered. These work very well:

- *'Parisienne':* Looks like radishes, tastes like carrots. This variety is easy to grow and if there's such a thing as an adorable carrot, it's this one.

'Parisienne' carrots

- 'Tonda di Parigi': Another choice for a radish-size carrot that resembles the 'Parisienne' carrots above, this one takes just sixty days and only grows about 2 inches long.

Another option is a type of carrot called 'Nantes' that has the tapered shape that's familiar to all carrot lovers, but is shorter and wider than traditional varieties, making it better for indoor growing. Try these:

- *'Shin Kuroda':* A Japanese variety that takes about seventy-five days to mature, but results in a tender carrot that's only about 3 to 5 inches long.
- *'Danvers Half Long':* If you have the container space for a 7-inch carrot, this is a nice choice since it's dependable and hearty.

'Nantes' family carrots

- *'Little Finger':* Although these take a bit longer to grow, they only grow about 3 inches long, which make them perfect for indoor gardens.

Trays, Pots, and Other Containers

Even with shorter varieties, carrots need ample room to grow, so use containers that are at least a foot deep, if not more. Even though the vegetables won't take up that space, their root system will use the room to develop properly.

You can opt for a rectangular container to mimic the look of carrots in a field, or utilize a round pot, which looks cool when all the carrot greens are fluffed up together. As with other crops, terra cotta pots are less ideal because they tend to draw moisture from the soil, but with a regular watering schedule, this is less important than it would be for something like lettuces.

When selecting a planter, make sure that it's thoroughly cleaned if you've grown plants in it previously. Even with old pots, it's possible to transfer diseases onto the new crop, and since carrots are root vegetables, they would be more affected by any contaminants that leach into the soil.

Prep Work

Carrots do well in loose soil, and even a small degree of compaction can result in stunted growth. Because of this, you might consider a soilless mix like compost and sand mixed together, or at least putting some vermiculite in your potting mix to allow for more drainage.

This may be a chance to try out coir bricks, if you haven't played around with those before. These bricks, made up of coconut fiber (called "coir") can be expanded to create a carbon-rich base beneath potting soil, or parts can be broken off and used to create a looser soil mix. As an added bonus, coir is great for compost piles, and is often used for vermiculture, so if your next step in gardening is creating your own worm bins, coir should be on your greenhouse shopping list.

Coir bricks are made of compressed coconut fiber. You can break off pieces and mix them with compost for a perfect carrot-growing medium.

Planting and Care

First Steps

Like radishes, carrots tend to do well when planted during cooler times of year like late spring or early fall, but in an indoor environment, they can thrive as long as the temp doesn't get too hot.

After creating your soil or soilless mix, fill your container and leave an inch of empty space at the top. Poke your finger into the planting medium where you'd like the carrots to go, about half an inch deep. Space the seed holes about 3 inches apart, if not more.

Drop two to three seeds into each hole, which will increase your chances of having at least one sturdy, hardy carrot in each spot. If more develop, you can simply thin them out and let the strongest one keep growing. Sprinkle soil or vermiculite on top of the holes, being careful not to press down when filling, since compaction could hinder germination.

Water thoroughly, so that the planting medium feels very wet but not flooded. Place pot in an area that gets at least six hours of light per day, usually in an area with some direct sunlight and some indirect. Carrots do well in shade, but also grow better with at least some partial sunlight.

Maintaining Growth

Some tips on getting carrots from seed to harvest:

- Keep the soil or soilless mix well watered. Because you've created a looser blend than for other vegetables, the carrots will probably need to be watered more often, especially during hotter days. Carrots can tolerate some dryness in the soil, but prefer a steady supply of moisture for better growing.
- If growth seems sluggish, you can apply fertilizer once a week for a few weeks, but this isn't necessary if growth is proceeding well.
- Thin out the carrots if they begin to seem crowded by simply plucking out the greens that are smaller than others. Be careful during the process, though, since you don't want to damage the roots of the remaining carrots.

Troubleshooting

Some common problems with carrots and potential solutions:

Greens Are Flopped Over into the Pot

Carrots need their greens to be upright, so take this concern seriously. Fortunately, there's an easy fix: simply "hill up" the greens by adding more soil around them and forming a larger base for them until they stand up. This tactic will also be helpful if carrot roots begin to appear too early, which can turn them green and bitter.

Whitish Spots Are Forming on the Leaves and/or Soil

Frequent watering helps carrot growth, but it can also lead to mildew formation, which is what's happening here. Carrots, in particular, can be prone to mildew because they need ample water, and mildew often forms in a field or garden after too much rain. All is not lost, though. You can either use a commercial antifungal spray or apply a natural spray made up of these ingredients:

- 1 gallon of lukewarm water
- 1 Tbsp baking soda
- 2 to 3 drops of mild liquid soap (such as Dr. Bronner's)
- 1 tsp of olive oil

Mix well, and put in a spray bottle, then mist the plant daily. The solution helps to tweak the pH balance on the surface of the leaves, which usually takes care of the mildew.

Harvesting and Preservation

Getting Ready to Pick

Much like radishes, carrots indicate when they're ready to be picked by "shouldering," which means they push up out of the soil with part of the vegetable showing. This is hugely helpful in determining the size of the carrot.

If they aren't shouldering, gently dig into the soil with your finger until you can feel the top of the carrot, and this will give you an idea of the size. If they're not ready, just replace whatever soil you've moved and check again in a few days. In some cases, carrots will shoulder too early and begin to turn green, and if this happens, hill up the soil around the carrot to prevent more of the carrot being exposed.

Once they're ready for harvest, just take hold at the base of the leaves and give a firm tug. It doesn't take much effort, and they tend to come out easily.

Storage Considerations

Carrots are well suited for long term storage, and they're a staple in many root cellars. The trick to storing them for weeks or even months is to refrain from washing them after harvest (save the scrub up for right before eating), since that can hasten spoilage. Also, if possible, arrange carrots so they aren't touching each other.

Whether you plan on short-term storage or a longer timeframe, remove the greens because they draw moisture away from the carrot and make the vegetable dry out faster. If properly stored, carrots can keep in the refrigerator up to three months.

Carrots, like other root vegetables, tend to "shoulder" as they mature, and this makes it easy to judge when they are ready for picking. A shoulder of about 1-inch diameter is a good range for most carrots.

Indoors or out, few veggies are more fun to harvest than carrots: especially if you like surprises.

KALE & CHARD

Much like lettuce, kale and chard are some of my favorite foods, and we grow plenty of them at the farm. Because they're such nutritional powerhouses, I also like growing them on a smaller level at home, and I tend to use a fair amount of both in my microgreens mixes.

Until we started farming, I wasn't aware of the breadth of varieties for both these hearty greens, since I usually saw only a few kinds of kale and two types of chard at my local co-op. But you'll find a beautiful array of options once you start traveling down the rabbit hole of seed catalog perusal, believe me.

Each has unique benefits when it comes to health, but they tend to have the same requirements for growing, which is why they're grouped here. Technically, I could also put collards into this category, and feel free to use these instructions if you want to add those to your indoor growing mix. But I've found that collards do best when they're allowed to grow to full maturity, which usually means leaves the size of dinner plates. That requires a mighty big container for an indoor space, but if you have a large planter and you're a collards lover, that would be a nice option for your indoor edibles mix.

All chard is attractive to a certain extent, but red chard (shown) and rainbow chard are particularly colorful and striking.

(OPPOSITE PAGE) In addition to their high nutritional value, kale and chard are beautiful plants with impressive structure. They make fine focal points in high-visibility spots.

Get Ready

Good Varieties for Indoor Growing

Kale, in particular, comes in an array of varieties, with some growing a few feet tall and others remaining as squat and sturdy as cabbage. For indoor growing, I tend to like the smaller varieties that still offer plenty of texture and color variation, like these:

- *'Dwarf Blue Curled':* There are a few "dwarf" varieties, and they work well inside because they don't take up too much space. This one, which takes about 55 days from seed to harvest, has a dense frill and a very slight bluish tint.

Curly kale stays small; look for dwarf varieties

- *'Red Russian':* Thanks to its mild flavor, this is a nice choice for adding raw to salads. The color is stunning, with purple stems and dark reddish green leaves.

'Red Russian' kale

- *'Lacinato':* Also known as Dinosaur, this variety seems to inspire intense devotion in its fans. I like it for the super durable leaves, which hold up nicely during cooking.

'Lacinato' (dinosaur kale)

With chard, I love the 'Rainbow' variety (also called 'Bright Lights') because the colors are so gorgeous. From neon yellow to delicate pink, the stems of the 'Rainbow' hold their colors even after cooking, making them a nice addition to dishes. Other varieties that are also good for indoor growing include:

- *'Peppermint':* I wish this was a minty-tasting chard because the weirdness of that combination would be worth trying. But in actuality, it's a variety that has pink and white striped stems. If you're harvesting at "baby" stage, it's only about thirty days from seed to harvest.

- *Orange or Yellow:* Unlike other types of vegetables, chard doesn't tend to have catchy names, apart from 'Fordhook Giant' or 'Silverado'; instead, they're identified by stem and vein color, but that can actually be helpful when choosing, since you can grow only orange, pink, red, or yellow varieties.

Yellow chard

'Bright Lights' chard

Trays, Pots, and Other Containers

Even though you're choosing smaller varieties of kale and chard, the plants still need plenty of room to stretch out, so this might be a good time to utilize a larger planter that you have on hand. I've attempted to seed one chard plant in a medium-sized pot and the results were mediocre; I had much better growth when using a large rectangular pot that fit well underneath my full-spectrum fluorescents.

Prep Work

When planting, aim for late spring or early fall. It's always tempting to plant in the winter so that you'll have chard in February, but even with plenty of light and warmth, the results tend to be spindly, and the germination is sluggish. Instead, planting in the early fall will allow the vegetables to establish before the cooler weather hits in earnest.

In terms of soil, standard indoor potting mix will work, and just make sure that there's adequate drainage. You can also blend some compost into the soil for added nutrition.

Planting and Care

First Steps

In order to get a nice amount of moisture throughout the soil before planting, mix your soil with some water until it has a damp, but not soaked, consistency. You can determine adequate water level by grabbing a handful and squeezing—if water runs in a steady stream, then it's too wet and you need to add more dry soil. If just a drop or two of water comes out, that's perfect.

Put the soil in your container (if you've mixed it elsewhere), leaving about an inch on top from the edge of the container.

Another nice trick for getting more moisture into the plants is to soak your seeds in lukewarm water for a few hours before planting. This will help boost the germination process, particularly in houses that tend to be dry.

Sow two or three seeds in holes about half an inch deep and at least 5 inches apart. Cover lightly with soil, and then mist the soil until it's moist but not saturated. Put the container in the sun or under a grow light.

Maintaining Growth

Here are some tips on getting your kale and chard from seed to harvest:

- If growth seems slow, add some nutrients by mulching the top of the plants with compost, coir, even grass clippings or dried leaves. You can also add natural fertilizer such as a kelp blend.

- Water when needed. Check the soil daily to see if it seems dry, and water if necessary. Don't water automatically, since you don't want the roots to stay damp continually, which can lead to rot.

Soak kale or chard seeds in lukewarm water for a couple of hours before planting.

Chard and kale both require good airflow, so don't pack them too tightly together and put a small fan out to create breeze around them.

Maintain good airflow. Kale and chard are high in antioxidants, but only because they have to contend with wind when they're outside, which creates stronger plant defenses. Mimic that natural environment by increasing airflow around the plants, and changing the "wind" direction occasionally. You don't want airflow to be so strong that it's making the plants flatten, but it should be robust enough that the plants need to work against it in order to grow heartier.

Troubleshooting

Some common problems with kale and chard and potential solutions:

**Germination Seems
to Be Taking a Long Time**

There can be several reasons why germination is sluggish for kale or chard. Your house might be too cold or too hot, or the plant could be situated too far from a light source. Try moving the light closer to the container, and also re-mist the soil with water, then cover it with plastic wrap to create a mini-greenhouse environment.

**The Plants Seem to Be
Crowding Each Other**

Thin out the weaker plants by either plucking them from the soil or by cutting the small leaves close to the top of the soil. The stronger plants will then have more room to grow, and you can eat the leaves you've removed.

Harvesting and Preservation

Getting Ready to Pick

Kale and chard can be harvested at any stage of growth, from petite green up to full leaf. I tend to harvest my indoor varieties when the leaves are about the size of my palm, as opposed to the size of my forearm, which is when I harvest varieties grown outdoors.

When harvesting, cut low on the plant to get some of the stem, since this part can be chopped up and used in stir fries, or quickly steamed to maintain crunchiness. Be sure to avoid the inner parts of the plant when harvesting, since this will be where new growth occurs, and snipping these leaves will hasten the plant's end.

Storage Considerations

Like lettuce, I tend to harvest kale and chard only when I'm about to eat it or juice it. If you need to store the leaves for a few days, though, simply put them in a plastic bag in your fridge's crisper drawer, or in a glass container if you're using the main part of the fridge. Since the higher shelves of a refrigerator aren't as cold as the lowest shelf, I store them there so they can stay crisp for longer.

SPINACH

Technically, spinach can come under the same category as kale and chard, but I decided to tweeze it out into its own section because it has a few unique requirements. Also, to emphasize its awesomeness.

When I was a kid, spinach was my most hated vegetable, by a huge degree. This may have been because we never had Brussels sprouts, but mostly it was because the spinach we had was the canned, clumpy kind that smelled like old, dirty underwear. There was an acrid tang to the aroma that transferred into the taste, and there was literally no amount of money I could have been promised in exchange for eating it.

Then, around the time I stopped eating snack food as a meal, I found out about real spinach—the kind with tender leaves, and it looked like a plant instead of a greenish clot. These days, I love growing spinach in part because I'm still amused by my dietary turn-around. The plant is often so hearty that it can produce for months, and the flavor is delicate, especially when steamed. So, I grow it indoors during the winter for its nutritional prowess, but also as a nod to that super picky kid—I have so much time I have to make up for with spinach.

(OPPOSITE PAGE) Spinach can be grouped pretty tightly for indoor growing.

Good Varieties for Indoor Growing

There are numerous varieties of spinach, but those designated as "baby leaf" tend to work best indoors because they're meant to be harvested at a small size. The leaves will tend to have a mild flavor with a nice bit of crunch that pairs well with salad greens. Here are a few varieties to consider:

- *'Catalina'*: This kind is the most popular for indoor growing, and for good reason. The deep green oval leaves are very flavorful and the variety is designed to grow quickly.

Baby leaf spinach ('Catalina')

- *'Emu'*: Unlike varieties like 'Catalina', with oval leaves, this one has pointed leaves, which make for a nice contrast.

'Emu' spinach

- *'Red Cardinal'*: This is a fun option for a color change, since it has red veins and stems and dark green leaves. With this one, the good news is that it's designed to be harvested at baby leaf stage, but the bad news is that it tends to have a shorter lifecycle than many other varieties.

Red varieties of spinach

- *'Red Kitten'*: If you want the red veins but crave a longer lifespan, go for this awesomely named variety; keep in mind, though, that it grows somewhat slower than 'Red Cardinal'.

Trays, Pots, and Other Containers

Spinach has a shallow root system, so you can use smaller pots if that's handy for you. They should be at least 6 inches deep, so in some cases, you can use the leftover trays that you might have used for microgreens or pea shoots, just be sure to scrub them thoroughly and let them dry completely before you replant in them.

I tend to like rectangular pots because they fit well on my shelves under my fluorescent lights, but I've seen many configurations for spinach, from growing a single plant in an old plastic tub to combining spinach with herbs in a larger container.

Prep Work

Spinach appreciates cooler weather, so aim for planting in early fall if possible so that the plants can establish before any major temperature drops. At our farm, we experimented with planting spinach in October and then covering it with reemay, a landscape fabric that lets light in but keeps bugs out. Even in a tough Minnesota winter, the spinach did great and we were able to harvest in early spring, after it "woke up" from its hibernation. Similarly, you can keep it going in your house during the winter if you live in a chilly climate, but it's best to get it germinating and growing before any major temperature variations.

In terms of soil, standard indoor potting mix will work, and just make sure that there's adequate drainage by adding some sand, coir, or vermiculite. You can also blend some compost into the soil for added nutrition.

The plastic oblong planter is perfect for a nice little indoor spinach patch.

Planting and Care

First Steps

In order to get a nice amount of moisture throughout the soil before planting, mix your soil with some water until it has a damp, but not soaked, consistency. You can determine adequate water level by grabbing a handful and squeezing—if water runs in a steady stream, then it's too wet and you need to add more dry soil. If just a drop or two of water comes out, that's perfect.

Put the soil in your container (if you've mixed it elsewhere), leaving about an inch on top from the edge of the container.

Sow two or three seeds in holes about half an inch deep and at least 5 to 8 inches apart. Cover lightly with soil, and then mist the soil until its moist but not saturated. Put the container in the sun or under a grow light.

You should begin to see germination in about seven to fourteen days, depending on variety and growing conditions.

Maintaining Growth

Here are some tips on getting your spinach from seed to harvest:

- Watch the temperature. Spinach doesn't do well in very warm conditions, so if your house is over 75 degrees, move the plant to a cooler spot.
- Water when needed. Check the soil daily to see if it seems dry, and water if necessary. Don't water automatically, since you don't want the roots to stay damp continually, which can lead to rot.

Poke holes about ½ inch deep for spinach seeds and plant two or three seeds per holes.

Instead of planting spinach from seed in your containers, you can start it outdoors or in a greenhouse and then transplant the small spinach plants when they are strong enough.

Troubleshooting

Some common problems with spinach and potential solutions:

The Spinach Just Started Growing, and Now It Has a Flower in the Center

This is called "bolting" and it's a sign that the plant is nearing the end of its life. Most likely, the timeframe for your spinach got significantly shortened because the plant got too hot. If other plants aren't bolting yet, move the planter to a cooler place and be sure to pick off any tall stems that look like they're about to flower. You can also detect signs of bolting when the spinach leaves taste more bitter than they did previously.

Germination Seems Uneven

Sometimes, several spinach plants in the same pot will germinate at different times, leaving "gaps" in the soil. Simply plant more seeds in those spaces, since they can catch up quickly. Since germination is usually fairly quick, they won't be far behind those that were planted the week before.

Leaves Are Wilted, Bruised, or Yellowing

Most likely, this is a sign of overwatering or of not enough nutrients. Try to "dry out" the plant for a day or two and when you resume watering, place the pot in a tray or sink filled with a few inches of water and remove it when you can see the soil on top begin to dampen. Sometimes, spinach pots can develop a "dead zone" inside where water flows around that area inside the pot, leaving it overly dry even though the soil on top shows adequate water.

If your spinach flowers that means it is bolting and it may already be too late to harvest it before the leaves become highly bitter. Some types of spinach, like the Malabar seen here, do have edible flowers.

Harvesting and Preservation

Getting Ready to Pick

Spinach can be harvested at any stage of growth, from petite green up to full leaf. If you've planted a baby leaf variety, harvest when the leaf is about 6 inches long.

When harvesting, cut low on the plant to get some of the stem, and be sure to avoid the inner parts of the plant when harvesting, since this will be where new growth occurs, and snipping these leaves will hasten the plant's end.

Storage Considerations

Spinach will keep for about a week in the refrigerator if properly stored. Don't wash the leaves until you're about to eat them, and wrap the spinach in plastic wrap, squeezing out as much air as you can. Unfortunately, cooked spinach doesn't store very well—it tends to turn into the glop I remember as a kid—but the plastic wrap tactic will at least keep your fresh spinach ready for cooking for a few days, if not longer.

(OPPOSITE PAGE) Spinach is adaptable and tough and can be moved around as you need. Avoid too much direct sunlight and any rooms that are over 75 degrees Fahrenheit for extended periods of time. Try putting some on top of the refrigerator and reserve the more visible spots for plants that need more maintenance or are prettier. (BELOW) Spinach leaves should be snipped off, not torn, near the base the stem. Take the outer leaves first to give the inner leaves a chance to grow.

IKEA

BEETS

Much like carrots and radishes, success with indoor growing for beets is often about variety selection. Root vegetables like these are all fairly similar in terms of root depth, so I tend to grow them in their own separate pots rather than trying to create a mini-farm in a single large container.

Beets are a fabulous addition to an indoor edible garden for many reasons. Nutritionally, they're astounding, since they're packed with potassium, iron, beta carotene, folic acid, and other vitamins and minerals. The ancient Romans used them as an aphrodisiac (not so surprising, since they contain significant amounts of boron, which is connected to the production of human sex hormones), and they've been used just as long for detoxification. Plus, you can eat the greens.

Beets are grown in-home most often as microgreens, but if you have the space and desire you can let them grow to maturity, too.

Because of their deep colors, beets also add a nice bit of variety to an indoor garden, especially one that might be leaning more toward greens like pea shoots and microgreens.

Good Varieties for Indoor Growing

Personally, I don't mind the dark red beets that stain cutting boards (and usually my shirt) when I slice into them for cooking. But some people avoid beets because they don't want to deal with this dramatic juice. Fortunately, there are options that let you avoid the issue entirely.

One quick note on variety: sometimes, farmers sell "baby beets" that are about half the size of other beets and often have fully-formed leaves. These aren't actually a type of beet, they're simply standard beets that have been thinned out of a bed so that other beets can grow larger. They're still delicious, just don't try looking for them as a seed variety.

- *'Chioggia':* This variety features pink-striped stems and an interior that has red rings, looking somewhat like a bulls-eye. They can grow fairly big, though, so if you're trying to stick to smaller containers, opt for a more modest beet type.

- *'Cylindra':* Also known as 'Formanova,' this beet forms a cylindrical, purple-tinged root that looks nothing like the beets that most people picture. It needs ample space, so if you want a candidate for your largest pot, consider this quirky variety.

- *'Touchstone Gold':* An orange-yellow exterior and bright yellow interior make this beet a beautiful addition to a garden. The tops can get tall, and the beet is only slightly smaller than a 'Chioggia,' but it's worth creating more space for such a stunner.

- *'Zeppo':* Here's a smaller beet, and at fifty days from seed to harvest, it's faster growing that many other varieties. They're fairly dependable when it comes to germination, but keep in mind that you might get the red juice when cutting them.

Trays, Pots, and Other Containers

Even with smaller varieties, beets need ample room to grow because their taproot (the thing that looks like a long rat's tail) can extend quite a bit into earth. Because of that, use containers that are at least 16 inches deep.

You can opt for a rectangular container to mimic the look of beets in a field, or utilize a round pot, which looks cool when all the red-veined greens are standing up together. As with other crops, terra cotta pots are less ideal because they tend to draw moisture from the soil, but with a regular watering schedule, this is less important than it would be for something like lettuces.

When selecting a planter, make sure that it's thoroughly cleaned if you've grown plants in it previously. Even with old pots, it's possible to transfer diseases onto the new crop, and since beets are root vegetables, they would be more affected by any contaminants that leach into the soil.

Prep Work

Beets do well in loose soil, so you might consider a soilless mix like compost and sand mixed together, or at least putting some vermiculite in your potting mix to allow for more drainage. I've had success with an indoor potting soil mix combined with some vermiculite,

and putting coir at the bottom of the pot.

Avoid using any larger materials when creating your soil mix, however. The beets will grow around even medium-sized rocks, resulting in some warped-looking vegetables.

Before seeding, add some fertilizer like a seaweed blend, or just a little compost tea, if you happen to create that at home or have that as an option at your local garden store. Compost tea works well for a wide variety of vegetables, especially for those that seem to be struggling. The solution has beneficial soil microbes that result from composted matter, and you only need a small amount for application. I often use either fish fertilizer or compost tea for stressed-out plants, or before seeding beets, because it provides a quick hit of nutrition without heavy fertilization.

Beets draw nutrients rather heavily so a little compost tea or other fertilizer is a good idea.

Planting and Care

First Steps

After creating your soil mix, fill your container and leave an inch of empty space at the top. Poke your finger into the planting medium where you'd like the beets to go, about half an inch deep. Space the seed holes about 3 inches apart, if not more.

Drop two to three seeds into each hole, since this will increase your chances of having at least one sturdy, hardy beet in each spot. If more develop, you can simply thin them out and let the strongest one keep growing. Sprinkle soil or vermiculite on top of the holes, being careful not to press down when filling, since compaction could hinder germination.

Water thoroughly, so that the planting medium feels very wet but not flooded. Place pot in an area with full sun.

Maintaining Growth

Here are some tips on getting your beets from seed to harvest:

- Water regularly—unlike some crops that should be watered when the soil is particularly dry, beets do well with a predictable watering schedule. This will help them to grow more quickly. Don't overwater, though. If greens begin looking yellowish, let the plant dry out a bit.
- Rotate your container if you have it in front of a window instead of under a light. Greens tend to lean toward the light source, which is fine if it's directly overhead, but can be stressful on the plant if it's always on one side of the pot.

Because of their broad leaves and tendency toward heliotropism, beets should be rotated by quarter- or half-turns regularly so they don't lean.

Troubleshooting

Some common problems with beets and potential solutions:

Beets Too Close to Each Other

At our farm, the beets always start out looking like a line of people trying to shop at a big box store the day after Thanksgiving. They're constantly pushing each other for space, and very often, we need to thin them not just once, but two or sometimes three times, depending on how large they're getting. Most likely, you'll experience similar crowding, and when that happens, gently pull out the weaker and smaller beet greens, and add them to a salad. When they're "harvested" at this stage, they're considered microgreens.

Greens Are Flopped Over into the Pot

Like carrots, beets do better when the greens are upright, so "hill up" the greens by adding more soil around them and forming a larger base for them until they stand up.

Abundant Greens, but Minimal Beet Growth

This can happen when too much nitrogen is in the soil. Most likely, you've been overfertilizing, so flush out some of the nitrogen by ceasing usage of that and watering regularly instead, making sure the pot has adequate drainage.

Beets Are Cracked or Split

With farming, this happens often, because it's an indication of uneven moisture levels. In other words, you get heavy rains, followed by near drought, and then heavy rains again. Beets are happiest with consistent water levels, and they split if they don't have that. This issue is less common with indoor gardening efforts, because you can control the frequency and amount of watering. If you're seeing splitting, look at your notes to see if you can refine your watering schedule.

Harvesting and Preservation

Getting Ready to Pick

Much like radishes and carrots, beets indicate when they're ready to be picked by "shouldering," which means they push up out of the soil with part of the vegetable showing. This is hugely helpful in determining the size of the beet.

If they aren't shouldering, gently dig into the soil with your finger until you can feel the top of the beet, and this will give you an idea of the size. If they're not ready, just replace whatever soil you've moved and check again in a few days. In some cases, beets will shoulder too early and begin to turn green, and if this happens, hill up the soil around the beet to prevent more of the beet being exposed.

Once they're ready for harvest, just take hold at the base of the leaves

If the shoulders of your in-home grown beets get this big, you will have triumphed. It is not easy, but it can be done.

and give a firm tug. It doesn't take much effort, and they tend to come out easily.

Storage Considerations

Beets store well for up to three weeks in the refrigerator, as long as you don't wash them first, which can quicken spoilage. Also, clip the leaves and store them separately, also unwashed, in a plastic bag in the crisper drawer.

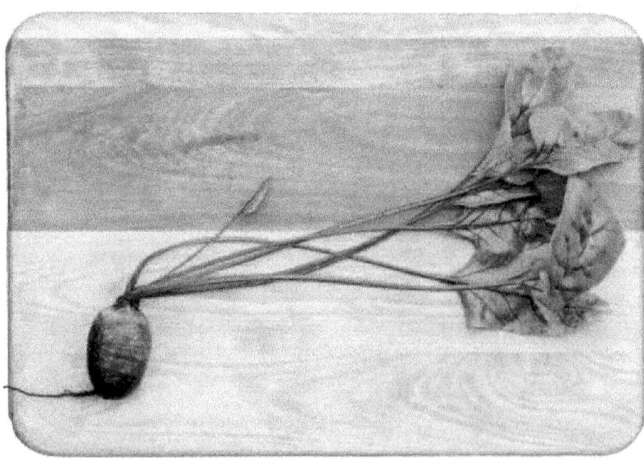

Don't forget about the greens. Many gardeners grow beets just for the greens, which have an earthy flavor and are prepared and consumed in much the same way as spinach, chard, or any other rugged green (turnip, mustard, etc.).

HOT PEPPERS

In my indoor growing ventures, I've had limited success with bell peppers, mainly because they require a higher degree of warmth and more light than everything else I'm growing.

As you may find with your own indoor gardening strategies, having one plant that demands more of your attention and is kind of a space-and-resources hog can make your gardening feel like it's taking up more time than you want to give. Personally, I like to set my schedule for indoor gardening—more hours in the winter, barely any in the summer—and having one vegetable that throws it all off is a primary candidate for getting booted from the grow space.

Hot peppers, on the other hand, are a different story. Some varieties grow to a nice, manageable size for a container, and although they do have unique needs when it comes to heat and watering, they're easily maintained.

Hot chile pepper plants generally fare well indoors and are well proportioned for most indoor kitchen gardens.

Get Ready

Good Varieties for Indoor Growing

Although it might seem that hot pepper plants have an especially shallow root system—they're dishearteningly easy to knock over or pull out of the ground by accident—there are several varieties that rely on extending their roots fairly deep into the soil. That's why it's particularly important to choose a variety that's better suited to indoor growing, unless you want to invest in larger containers. These tend to work well for an indoor garden:

- *'Firecracker':* With this variety, peppers grow straight upward rather than hanging down, creating a firework-type of effect. Peppers turn from green to yellow to red while maturing.

'Firecracker' chile pepper

- *'Habanero':* With a characteristic orange color and a very pungent aroma, this is one of the hottest peppers you can grow. If you're sensitive to capsaicin, which gives peppers their heat, you may want to use gloves when harvesting and handling this one.

Habanero pepper

- *'Hungarian Hot Wax':* Particularly good for making pickled peppers, this variety produces robust fruit that changes from yellow to red, and is spicy but not my-mouth-is-on-fire hot.

'Hungarian Hot Wax' pepper

Trays, Pots, and Other Containers

Like many other plants, hot peppers will do better in plastic than in terra cotta pots, because the clay will dry out the soil mix faster than the plastic. Considering that the peppers will require more heat and moisture than many other plants you might be growing, using terra cotta will thwart your efforts.

When selecting a planter, make sure that it's thoroughly cleaned if you've grown plants in it previously. Even with old pots, it's possible to transfer diseases onto the new crop.

Glazed ceramic pots work very well with pepper plants from a design standpoint.

Prep Work

All indoor plants need attention when it comes to water, light, and heat, but hot peppers are especially finicky about these three factors. Make sure you have either a sunny spot by a south-facing window or adequate grow lights. The lights should be positioned only about 6 inches above the plant while it germinates, and should be left on for fourteen to sixteen hours per day.

In terms of soil, standard indoor potting mix will work, and just make sure that there's adequate drainage by adding some sand, coir, or vermiculite. You can also blend some compost into the soil for added nutrition.

Planting and Care

First Steps

With hot peppers, you can speed up germination time by tweaking the planting process, starting with getting moisture into the seeds. Follow these steps:

- Keep the container or bag in an area that's warm but not hot. In my house, this is on a shelf under our butcher block that's near the stove. If it's cold in the house, I might use a germination mat and put the container on that.
- Check the seeds after a few days, and if they seem puffed up then you're ready to plant. Sometimes they might even be starting to sprout, which is a great head start.

In order to get a nice amount of moisture throughout the soil before planting, mix your soil with some water until it has a damp, but not soaked, consistency. You can determine adequate water level by grabbing a handful and squeezing—if water runs in a steady stream, then it's too wet and you need to add more dry soil. If just a drop or two of water comes out, that's perfect.

Put the soil in your container (if you've mixed it elsewhere), leaving about an inch on top from the edge of the container.

Dampen two paper towels and place your seeds in a single layer across one of them, putting the other dampened paper towel on top.

Sow each seed about half an inch deep and at least 2 inches apart. Cover lightly with compost, and then mist the soil until it's moist but not saturated. Put the container in the sun or under a grow light.

You should begin to see germination in about one to six weeks, depending on variety and growing conditions.

Maintaining Growth

Here are some tips on getting your peppers from seed to harvest:

- Water thoroughly after the peppers germinate. Peppers thrive with regular watering, and you should mist or water when the soil is just beginning to look dry.

- Check airflow so that there's circulation, but not an indoor wind tunnel. For a few hours a day, turn on a small fan in the area, set on low. This will help to mimic outdoor conditions, but you don't want to bring down the temperature of the room too much.

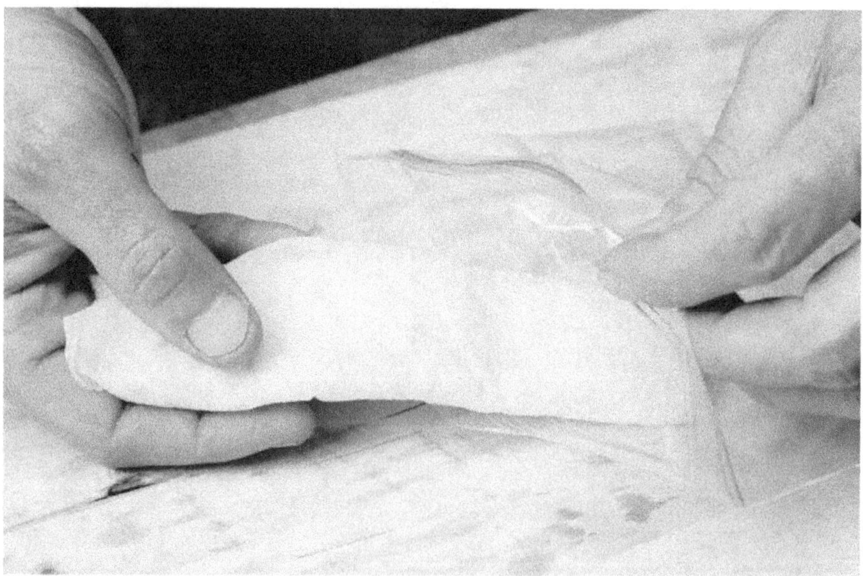

Put the seeds and paper towels into a plastic bag that can be sealed or a plastic container with a tight-fitting lid.

Troubleshooting

Some common problems with hot peppers and potential solutions:

Growth Seems Sluggish

Check your seed packet for seed-to-harvest maturity dates first, since peppers can vary widely in terms of growth timeframes. If it's off track, make sure that you're not placing the plants near areas that experience temperature fluctuations, such as a countertop under a heating vent or an air conditioning vent. Even placing the plant near an outside door that brings in cold air occasionally can cause the plant to slow its growth.

Germination Isn't Working, Even With the Paper Towel Method

Sometimes, pepper seeds can be fussy. In that case, it might be time to invest in a heat mat, which can be purchased at any garden store. These rectangular mats look like tiny heating pads, but they don't get as hot. If I'm experiencing slow germination times, especially in the winter, I place the pot on this type of mat and wait a few days—usually, the mat will heat the soil enough to foster growth. The heat is so minimal that you can put the mat on any surface, too; I usually put mine on a wooden counter, without any fear of scorching it.

Harvesting and Preservation

Getting Ready to Pick

Picking chili peppers off your own indoor plant has got to rank as one of the happiest experiences of home gardening. Depending on variety, you're likely looking at a cheery, brightly colored pepper that will taste amazing. Keep in mind that peppers will start off as green and then will gradually transition to a color if that's part of the variety you've chosen. If you're growing

When red chili peppers are bright red, snip them as they are needed with scissors. Avoid plucking them off the plant.

a type that stays green, you can check for "doneness" by gently squeezing the pepper—if it's rock solid, then it's not ready, but if it has some give to it, then you can harvest.

The best way to harvest is to clip the pepper close to the stem, rather than plucking them off, which can sometimes yank the plant along with it.

Storage Considerations

Peppers will store nicely in the refrigerator for at least a week, especially if you don't wash them first. They also dry exceedingly well with a food dehydrator or in the oven. When we have a bumper crop of peppers, I dry a bunch of them and then vacuum seal them to use later for chili or stew.

Red chili peppers, and many other types of peppers, dry readily in many environments, including most kitchens. They also look great, so don't be afraid to have some fun using them in your décor.

POTATOES

I n many cases, potatoes grow so well outside and store so beautifully that growing them indoors is more of a jaunty experiment than a practical venture. However, I'm a fan of taking on any kind of experiment, especially if it's jaunty.

Sometimes, indoor growing can be an advantage for potatoes, too. In our fields, we have to fight potato bugs on a yearly basis, and because we're big believers in organic practices and natural pest management control, that tends to mean that I squish them instead of spray them. Bright orange and fat as woodticks, potato bugs leave me with stained hands and a slightly nauseated feeling. But at home, I can just enjoy watching the potato plant's progress without the dread of "squashing day."

Also, there's a certain satisfaction that comes with knowing you're growing potatoes in your basement. It feels like being a modern pioneer.

Potatoes, believe it or not, can be grown in pots indoors.

Good Varieties for Indoor Growing

Farmers and gardeners rely on "seed potatoes" for planting, but that term doesn't mean that these potatoes are any different than the type you eat. In fact, many farmers (including us) put aside their best potatoes during harvest—which often means the ones with the most eyes and seem especially firm and hearty—and use those for the next planting.

Theoretically, you could also go into the grocery store and choose a bag of potatoes and call those your seed stock. However, this is usually a less-ideal solution because most potatoes, even many that are organic, are treated with anti-sprouting agents that extend their shelf life. Those supermarket potatoes might sprout at some point, but to grow the best potatoes possible, buy some potatoes that were specifically developed to be used as seed.

Because of their small size, fingerling potatoes can be a good indoor growing choice.

When researching your options (see Resources in the back for some choices), here are a couple factors to consider:

- Keep in mind that depending on your state, you may not be able to order the potatoes during certain months. This is because seed potatoes rot quickly if they're allowed to freeze, so seed companies won't ship them to colder climates if there's a chance that they'll get spoiled.
- Seed potatoes can run out once summer approaches. This makes sense, since most of these potatoes are harvested in early October and then are ordered by farmers and gardeners over the winter and early spring. By June, and sometimes even by April, the pickings get slim. So, plan ahead.
- One pound of seed potatoes will result in about 10 to 15 pounds of potatoes. It doesn't take much to make a pound of potatoes, so when ordering, lean toward the conservative side.
- Much like other indoor crops, choosing smaller varieties tends to work well. I've had success with fingerling varieties like 'Russian Banana' and 'French Fingerling', as well as more petite options like 'Mountain Rose', 'Rio Grande', or 'All Blue'.
- Compared to other crops you might be growing indoors, potatoes take a long time, especially if you've got trays of fast-sprouting wheatgrass and microgreens in the mix as comparison. The quickest timeframe you can get is about seventy days, but usually, you're looking at about four months. They don't require much maintenance at all, so it's not like you have to tweak your vacation schedule to grow them, but planning ahead is helpful so you can anticipate harvesting.

Containers

Here's your chance to use your biggest pot or container. Some people have used 5-gallon buckets with holes drilled in the bottom, or special potato growing bags that are fashioned out of heavy felt that can be easily moved around.

Whatever you choose, make sure that there's adequate drainage options, and that the pot is in an area where the water can drain easily. You'll be using a fair amount of water during the initial watering period and when you do maintenance watering, so placing the pot in a spot where you have easy water access and a drain is helpful—for my setup, the area near my laundry sink in the basement has proved to be ideal.

Prep Work

The main preparation for seeding potatoes is cutting and sprouting. For some smaller potatoes with only one "eye," this isn't a necessary step, but for the majority of seed potatoes, this strategy helps prevent diseases and ensures a heartier crop. Here are the steps:

Wash potatoes to remove dirt and debris; this is an especially important step if buying non-organic potatoes, because you want to remove any pesticide residue before planting.

Wash the seedling potatoes well.

Cut the seedlings into small pieces.

- Cut each potato into pieces that include at least one eye per piece. An "eye" is the indentation where a potato will sprout eventually.
- Set potatoes aside for at least a week before planting. The cut side should be allowed to toughen up, in a process also called scabbing. The eyes will begin to sprout, and this is a sign that the potato is ready to plant.
- Alternately, you can employ a method that's often used for teaching kids about plant growth: put four toothpicks around the potato chunk, about halfway between top and bottom. Put the potato eye-side down in a glass jar of water, with the toothpicks preventing the potato from submerging completely. Put the jar in a sunny spot, and change the water if it begins to look cloudy. Roots will sprout in about a week. This method can speed up sprouting if that's what you want, but you won't get the scabbing that helps with disease control.

In terms of soil, you can use indoor potting mix for vegetables, and mix in vermiculite or sand to help with drainage. Resist any urge to include outdoor garden soil in the mix, even if it's rich with compost and other nutrients. You don't want to take the chance that you'll bring in pests from outdoors.

Planting and Care

First Steps

Fill the pot or container about a third full of your soil mix. As the plant grows, you'll need to keep adding soil, so it's best to stay minimal with the amount at the beginning, even if it looks like the pot is mainly empty.

Place the potato chunks about 6 inches apart, and 3 inches deep, with root side down. Because the plants will need room to grow, it's best to put the seed potatoes at least 6 inches from the edge of the pot as well.

Cover the potatoes with about 3 inches of soil, and water them thoroughly, until water begins running out of the drainage holes in the bottom.

Maintaining Growth

When the plant has grown about 6 inches above the surface (about one to three weeks after planting) add more soil to the pot without completely covering the new growth. When the stem reaches the level of the top of your pot, add soil again and hill it around each stem. This helps to ensure that the potatoes will grow more deeply under the soil and won't be subjected to sunlight, which would cause them to turn green.

Green potatoes, while they sound colorful and charming, are mildly toxic because they contain a substance called solanine, which occurs when the plant feels threatened. The length of exposure to light, and the intensity of the light, can raise the level of solanine, with the highest concentration located in the potato's skin. This whole process can happen when the potato grows too close to the soil surface, or is stored long-term in an area with even low light levels. If you don't spot any green tint, you'll know when solanine is present because your potatoes have a bitter aftertaste. Prevent the issue by being diligent about hilling up the potatoes so they're well protected from light.

Keep the container well watered, but not soaking. The soil doesn't have to be particularly damp, but you should have the potatoes on a consistent watering schedule to foster more growth.

Troubleshooting

Some common problems with potatoes and potential solutions:

Plants Don't Come Up After Planting Seed Pieces

If you've taken a chance on using supermarket potatoes instead of certified seed potatoes, you may be thwarted in your growing. Also, if you planted the seed pieces before they sprout, they'll take longer to fully establish.

There Are Cute Little Yellow and Black Beetles on the Leaves

Evil takes many forms, and this is one of them. These are Colorado potato beetles, and you need to pick them off before they destroy your plants. You can squish them if you're feeling resentful, or simply throw them into some soapy water, where they'll expire. To make sure that you've gotten the eggs as well, cut up some basil leaves and let them steep in about a cup of water for a few days. Strain, put in a mister and thoroughly spray the leaves.

The Plants Are Staying Green Even Though It's Past the Maturity Date

This is probably the only instance in growing when you want dead, dry leaves instead of vibrant green ones. If this is happening, then it's likely that your grow space is too warm. Potatoes do best with cool nights of below 55 degrees, and even if you can't achieve that in your house, move the potatoes to the coolest spot in the house to see if it helps.

Harvesting and Preservation

Getting Ready to Pick

Depending on your potato variety, you'll be able to harvest after two to four months from planting. If you harvest closer to two months, you'll have "new potatoes," which have a thinner skin than the mature stage. That means they don't store for very long, but they do have a fresh, creamy taste that's delicious.

You can tell when potatoes are ready because there are usually very small-looking potatoes on the vines/stems, and the stems themselves will dry up and look terrible. When I first started growing potatoes, I always thought I was doing something wrong, but then I'd get a gorgeous little crop. Then I learned that the stem dies off as part of the maturation process, and it's about two to three weeks after they shrivel up that you can harvest the mature potatoes.

To dig them up, you can simply pull up on the stem and you'll see a string of potatoes, as well as the original seed potato, also called the "mother." This potato chunk will be soft and pretty gross and should be discarded. But the others can be collected and stored. Be sure to dig through the soil to make sure you haven't missed any potatoes that may have dropped off during harvest.

Picking the potatoes can make a bit of a mess—if you can move your plant outdoors it's not a bad idea.

Storage Considerations

If you plan to store potatoes for quite a while, place them in a dry spot out of direct sun, like in a shady patio or a garage. This will help them dry out before storage. Then place them in a cool, dry, dark place like a basement; usually, a mesh or burlap sack is ideal because it allows the vegetables to "breathe" while being stored.

No matter how long you plan on storing them, refrain from washing them between harvest and storage, and wash them only just before preparing them for cooking. This will keep the potatoes from potential rot while in storage.

TOMATOES

I've saved tomatoes for last because, in many cases, they feel like an extra credit project. Some gardeners have insisted to me that you simply can't grow tomatoes—viable, tasty ones, anyway—indoors because much of what they need is outdoors. For example: bees.

Pollination through the use of bees provides a major boost. After all, tomatoes are a fruit, and like many other fruits, they rely on cross pollination to increase the quality and abundance of the harvest. But you can game the pollination process (more on that later) if you're truly dedicated to indoor tomatoes.

Usually, even though I am ridiculously in love with tomatoes, I tend to leave them out of my indoor garden because I find them fussy. But then, when I bring them back in, I do have that moment of elation that comes with seeing a tiny green tomato that will eventually transition into a bright little treat.

Smaller tomatoes, such as cherry tomatoes (ABOVE) or bush-type (OPPOSITE PAGE) will do fine indoors if they get suitable amounts of light, wamth, moisture, and air movement.

Get Ready

Good Varieties for Indoor Growing

I'd like to say that I've grown palm-sized, juicy slicer tomatoes that dangle like coconuts in my kitchen, even with the snow going sideways outside. But my attempts at larger tomatoes have sputtered, so instead I stick with what I've found the most successful: cherry tomatoes and small varieties. Here are some favorites:

- 'Yellow Pear': This is a cheery, bright yellow heirloom variety that makes for a nice contrast with red and orange cherry tomatoes; plus, its pear shape is delightful.

'Yellow pear' tomato

- 'Pink Ping Pong': named for the size of the fruit, this cherry tomato doesn't actually get pink, but does have a slightly lighter reddish color.
- 'Tommy Toe': Originating from the Ozark mountains, this heirloom has high disease resistance and tends to yield copious amounts of tomatoes.

- 'Alaska': This is a nice pick for cooler climates, and it hails from Russia originally; an early producer, the tomato plant yields larger cherry tomatoes.
- 'Cream Sausage': A quirky tomato that's fun to grow, because it's bushy and so doesn't need trellising; also, the tomatoes are long and come to a point at the end, so they resemble peppers.

There are so many more—tomatoes, particularly heirlooms, come in hundreds of varieties, each with their own distinctive characteristics.

One important note is to look at determinate versus indeterminate varieties. The former means that the plant has been developed to reach a specific height and number of tomatoes per plant. They tend to be bushier and therefore don't need as much trellising or staking.

One drawback to determinates is that the tomatoes all ripen at the same time, so you don't have the ongoing fruit development that you'd see with inderminates, which produce fruit until they're killed by frost. Indeterminates are like the grab bag of the tomato world—you don't know what you're going to get in terms of height, fruit amount, or life cycle, but that's part of the fun.

Containers and Trellis Systems

Tomatoes do well with plenty of space for root growth, so opt for large containers and pots. These bigger containers also give you an opportunity to do more with staking and trellising, which is important for healthy plant growth. I've seen some successful grow systems that use 5-gallon buckets, which are handy because they can be easily moved. Any smaller than that size and you'll likely cramp the roots as they're trying to establish.

At this point, do I even have to mention the importance of drainage? Or of drilling holes in those 5-gallon buckets? If my editor would have allowed it, I may have been tempted to title this book *The Importance of Drainage: Indoor Growing for People Who Have Appropriate Pots for the Task*. Seriously, though, by now I'm sure you get it—drainage is awesome.

For a trellis system, I've seen all kinds of strategies, from a yardstick stuck into the soil with twine holding the plant to an elaborate grid-type plastic trellis that allowed for intensive support and attached to a "self-watering" pot.

Many people on a budget (like myself) do well with the standard tomato plant cage, which is often under $10 (and sometimes under $5) at garden stores. This triangular or round cage is about 3 to 4 feet high, made of wire, and can easily be stuck into any planter. Because it has several concentric rings, you can weave your growing tomato stems inside of it and tie them gently to the rings or sides.

With its compact cage and self-watering pot, this small patio tomato is all set to move indoors.

Prep Work

Unless you have a greenhouse space that you can outfit with some serious grow lights, it's best to utilize natural sunlight for tomatoes. This usually means finding the biggest south-facing window in your house and getting the tomatoes as close to full sun as possible. If you live in more southern climates, you may want to opt for an east-facing or even north-facing window.

If it's the middle of winter and you're barely getting enough sun yourself, then supplement the anemic natural light with some full-spectrum fluorescents. Dedicate at least two of these to your tomatoes, and place them close to the plants—usually no farther than a foot away.

In terms of soil, a good indoor potting soil will work, but be sure to increase the nutrient density with compost or other fertilizer. Also, help with drainage by putting some rocks or pebbles in the bottom of the pot so water won't sit inside the soil, leading to root rot.

Planting and Care

First Steps

You have a couple choices with how to establish tomato plants. You can start them from seed, but keep in mind that this tends to take quite a while and indeterminate varieties will only begin flowering when they're at least 3 feet high.

If you do begin from seed, consider using much smaller pots for the first stages of germination, since this will help to create a "root ball" and lead to a healthier, more robust plant. Simply put a seed into a small pot, about 2

In-home tomato plants can be started indoors too.

inches deep, cover with soil, and water consistently until you see growth.

As the plant begins to expand, transplant to a medium-sized container that will support the growth and put a small stick or ruler in the soil if you need to do a mini-trellis. After more growth, do one more transplant session to the larger container where you plan to have the plant for the rest of its life cycle. Each time you transplant be sure to water thoroughly—transplanting is often traumatic to a plant and it requires extra watering and care to recover from the shock.

You can also start your indoor tomatoes from cuttings, using outdoor plants at the end of the summer. Just snip a branch from a variety in your garden (or, with permission, someone else's garden) and strip off all the leaves except one on top. Put the stem in a jar of water and place in a window that gets plenty of sun. Roots will begin to form from the lower part of the stem, and once you see a few inches of root growth, put the stems in the large container, burying most of them but leaving the top leaves exposed.

Finally, you can simply buy transplants from a garden center. I promise, this isn't cheating. I like to call it a "head start" instead. Tomatoes take time, fertilization, water, and care to grow from tiny sprout to firmly established plant, and when I have a ton of other plants growing and just don't want to take the time and effort to nurture tomato plants along, getting some healthy, beautiful transplants from my locally owned garden center seems like a perfect strategy.

Tomato seedlings are cheap and reliable, but they are only available for a short time in the spring in most areas.

Maintaining Growth

As the plants begin establishing and getting larger, here are some strategies for fostering more growth:

- Hand pollination by gently shaking the plant's flowers daily; some people go beyond this tactic and use a paintbrush to "vibrate" the flowers. Either method is helpful, because it mimics the action of a bee or other pollinator. It's also fun to research different indoor pollination methods because people are very creative and come up with some surprising tactics, like using ostrich feathers, tuning forks set for middle C (seriously), or an electric shaver. Many people report particularly good results with an electric toothbrush, using the handle instead of the brush, because it shakes the flower as it dislodges the pollen.

- Keep proper airflow. Also an aid to pollination, and a generally good health booster is air circulation, so make sure that your growing space has a fan directed toward it. I use a rotating fan since that replicates that occasional breezes that would occur outside, as opposed to setting a fan to blow directly on the plant at all times, which could cause stress eventually.

- Create a natural day and night. Although tomatoes love sun, they also need to rest in order to grow properly, much like any other plant. So if you're utilizing growing lights, be sure to simulate a day by turning lights on at sunrise and off at sunset. If you're in northern climates during the winter, you may want to create a longer day for the tomatoes by extending your "day" for them by an extra few hours. This is where a timer can come in handy.

- Water consistently. Just like they love sun, tomatoes also appreciate regular watering. The soil in your container should be damp but not soaked, and it's likely that you'll have to water every few days, depending on the dryness of your house's air.

- Watch for insects like aphids, spider mites, and whiteflies. These are common in indoor spaces and can cause serious damage to your tomatoes. Either place sticky insect traps near the tomatoes or employ a soapy spray that consists of mild soap (like Dr. Bronner's) diluted in water and put into a spray bottle.

Troubleshooting

Some common problems with tomatoes and potential solutions:

Leaves Look Slightly Yellowed and Growth Seems Slow

When tomatoes seem to be struggling, they rebound nicely with some fertilizer application, particularly kelp and bone meal. Tomatoes are "heavy feeders," which means they need plenty of nutrients, and even with compost mixed into your soil, it's likely you'll have to add some fertilization along the way. When leaves begin to yellow, it's often a major sign of either nutrient deficiency or overwatering.

Tomatoes Have Black Areas on the Bottom That Look Burned

This is called blossom-end rot, and although it looks fairly serious, it's not a disease and can be controlled. The condition is sometimes caused by a calcium deficiency brought on by an uneven watering schedule. In the field, we see this problem when it rains heavily and then we're hit by drought. Another factor might be excess nitrogen, so if you're overfertilizing, you might see this form on several tomatoes. Fortunately, if you catch this early, you can correct the issue by keeping the soil at a consistent moisture level, and also by mulching— just cover the top of the soil with straw, available at any garden store, which helps to keep moisture in the soil.

Dark Spots on the Leaves

Another major thorn in the side of tomato growers is this fungal problem, known as "blight." For some home gardeners, blight takes out their tomato plants every season, and they try planting in new places to alleviate the issue. When growing indoors, it's easier to spot blight early and try containment methods. First, make sure you're not getting any water on the leaves or touching the plants when they're wet. Don't mist the plant, ever, as this will worsen the problem. Instead, pick off the affected leaves and destroy them. Increase air circulation to keep the leaves as dry as possible. If the issue is extensive, consider using a spray like copper fungicide, which is appropriate for use on organic plants. In addition to early blight, the spray also tackles powdery mildew, black spots, and downy mildew.

Fruit Developing Cracks

Here's another indication of uneven watering. See the answer above for strategies that will help alleviate the problem.

Harvesting and Preservation

Getting Ready to Pick

Nothing could be easier—just pluck the ripe fruit and see if you can resist popping the fruit in your mouth immediately. Ripeness will depend on variety, but expect your tomatoes to go through several color variations as they ripen, from green to vibrant color.

Storage Considerations

Tomatoes do well on the counter for a few days, especially if you need them to ripen more, which they'll continue to do even off the vine. Just don't put tomatoes in the fridge (unless you've turned them into salsa) because it significantly impacts the texture and flavor of the fruit.

Picking tomatoes is easy: just twist and pull.

VARY YOUR CROP MIX

Much like experimentation with herbs and microgreens, indoor crops can range widely, thanks to the breadth of varieties for each vegetable and fruit. After setting up a grow space and trying out a few favorites like carrots and radishes, you might explore the option of greater expansion.

In my experience, a success tends to kick off another scramble through seed catalogs, pondering whether I could nurture some dwarf fruit trees, for example, or edible flowers. Often, I broaden my experience by trying different varieties of a particular vegetable that's flourished well in my setup. In addition to a 'French Breakfast' radish, for example, I might utilize a deeper pot and see if 'Purple Plum' radishes can thrive as well.

It's also helpful to know that some vegetables are simply ill-suited for indoor growing on a small scale. They might be fine in a greenhouse, but that's an environment with carefully controlled humidity and temperature, commercially available lights, plenty of maintained and directed airflow, and frequent applications of fertilizer. Also, greenhouse managers work full-time to tweak all these components based on what they observe for eight hours (or more) per day.

For most people, myself included, it's far easier to stick to options that can be done on a smaller scale with minimal maintenance and cost. For many, that will mean tried-and-true crops like lettuces and carrots instead of field-loving options like cabbage, artichokes, or squash.

Fortunately, the varieties within the indoor-happy crops are wide ranging, from various spinach picks to heirloom cherry tomatoes. Start with a few that you'd love to see on your plate, and let the indoor growing venture expand from there.

Conclusion

Now Go Inside and Play

In this book, I've covered many options that have worked for me in terms of indoor gardening, but ultimately, it will be up to you to play around with your own mix of edible projects. Maybe you'll grow carrot microgreens instead of carrots, or you'll focus only on lettuces because you and your pet rabbit both appreciate a just-harvested plate of greens. See every success as an opportunity to open the door just a little bit more, and understand the power of setbacks.

Sometimes—more often than I'd like, certainly—I'll embark on a plan that doesn't work, and I'm back to feeling humbled. But I just jot down the results of my experiments and move on to other options. Will the 'White Beauty' radish be different? Could I pull off a watermelon radish even though it's so much larger than what I've planted in the past? These are the kinds of questions that leave me looking dreamy and distracted when I'm standing in line at the greenhouse, buying more coconut coir or fish fertilizer solution.

I've come to appreciate those daydream moments, because it means that I'm still curious and still open to the adventure. In gardening, and especially in indoor gardening with its tricky nuances, it can be easy to feel defeated sometimes. Despite all my cheerleading throughout this book, I've experienced plenty of frustration when I see mold, aphids, or crumpled leaves. The toughest moments are those when I look at a pot of soil mix and know that there's supposed to be a sweet little sprout poking up through vermiculite, and instead I have nothing.

But I comfort myself with the realization that this is all a work-in-progress, and that adaptability and flexibility are attributes to inform not only my gardening, but also my outlook on practically everything. When I think that way, I see my little indoor garden as a symbol of all that I want to cultivate in my life: nourishment, care, awareness, and joy.

Revel in that burst of pride that comes with seeing a plant begin to sprout up from the soil, and appreciate that feeling as it carries through all the way to the moment you serve it as part of a meal. In so many ways, gardening nourishes us, it not only creates a connection between ourselves and our food, but also to our communities and our planet.

Resources

This guide to indoor growing is meant to be a starting point for any new gardening effort, especially for those who haven't tried any indoor edibles before. There are tons of wonderful resources out there, from seed companies to mushroom spawn providers, that can expand your expertise and provide a wealth of in-depth information. Here are some of my favorites:

Seeds & Supplies

Johnny's Selected Seeds

www.johnnyseeds.com

This company is a treasured resource among farmers and gardeners, and for good reason. The site has videos, planting guides, herb growing charts, seed charts, and interactive tools. They also have an extensive collection of microgreen blends, which I've found particularly helpful and affordable.

High Mowing Seeds

www.highmowingseeds.com

If you're looking for non-GMO, all-organic seeds, this is a great resource. They have a wide range of vegetables and herbs, as well as a blog about growing practices, food preservation, and other topics.

Seeds of Change

www.seedsofchange.com

Another strong choice for organic seeds, this site also has a nice collection of tools and supplies, including wooden planter boxes and "yield pots" which are lightweight, durable, and breathable options for an indoor garden.

Seed Savers Exchange

www.seedsavers.org

This nonprofit organization is focused on saving and sharing heirloom seeds, and reading through the catalog is always compelling, because they share little stories about where the seeds originated. They also provide very clear instructions about planting, and tips for better growing.

Sprouts

Sproutpeople

www.sproutpeople.com

This is a powerhouse of a site for sprout enthusiasts. Not only do they stock over one hundred varieties of seed, but they also have sprouting kits, sprouters, juicers for wheatgrass, and other products. Best of all, they have "Sprout School," a section on the site that covers every topic from seed storage to harvesting.

Mumm's Sprouting Seeds
www.sprouting.com
Put together by a farming family, this
company has been selling organic
sprouting seed for over thirty years. In
addition to about fifty seed options, the
site offers sprouting equipment, books,
and information on growing issues.
Particularly nice is a section marked
as "Very Easy to Sprout" seeds, which
includes mixes that will appeal to first-
time sprouters.

With these sites and other sprouting and seed sites, it's also easy to find
microgreens and wheatgrass for sale.

Mushrooms

Field & Forest
www.fieldforest.net
Offering certified organic spawn and
tools, this site is also packed with information, and has a very useful beginner's
section. A video series on the site covers
shiitake log inoculation, wine cap iden-
tification, and thimble spawn usage.

Fungi Perfecti
www.fungi.com
First of all, this company's name is
fantastic, like something out of *Flash
Gordon*. It offers a variety of mushroom
kits and very helpfully tags them with
a growing difficulty rating. For example, its pink oyster mushroom patch
is considered easy to grow, while its
nameko mushroom patch is much
more challenging.

Mushroom Adventures
www.mushroomadventures.com
Another good purveyor of mushroom
kits, this company features popular
mushrooms like buttons, Portabellas,
crimini, and oysters. Check out the
"experiments" part of the site, where
they chronicle their attempts to grow
unusual varieties.